FROM INSPIRATION TO ACTIVISM
A PERSONAL JOURNEY THROUGH OBAMA'S PRESIDENTIAL CAMPAIGN

MARY LANG SOLLINGER

LITTLE CREEK PRESS
AND BOOK DESIGN

Mineral Point, Wisconsin

Little Creek Press®
A Division of Kristin Mitchell Design, Inc.
5341 Sunny Ridge Road
Mineral Point, Wisconsin 53565

Book Design and Project Coordination:
Little Creek Press®

First Edition
March 2020

Printed in the United States of America

For more information or to order books:
visit www.littlecreekpress.com

Library of Congress Control Number: 2020902280

ISBN-13: 978-1-942586-76-0

Some names and identifying details have been
changed to protect the privacy of individuals.

For more information go to: www.mlsollinger.com
or email: mlsollinger@gmail.com

To my father, who inspired me to do something unexpected, for my country, as he did. He was always clear about what was right and wrong and quietly acted on it. He lived and taught me to "leave your place a little bit better than how you found it."

O

To the tens of thousands of volunteers, ordinary people, who for the love of our country, did extraordinary things during the past presidential elections.

PRAISE FOR MARY LANG SOLLINGER'S
From Inspiration to Activism: A Personal Journey through Obama's Presidential Campaign

❝Mary Lang Sollinger's book reflects a deep conviction she and I share: civic engagement is a unique power, and through action, we can harness that power to effect change. My involvement with the Obama campaign in 2008 was one of the highlights of my life, and this book does a good job of capturing why."

—Virginia Senator Tim Kaine

❝As a key player on many successful campaigns and political movements, Mary Lang Sollinger has a keen understanding of what it takes to win. Her book offers a great insight into the early rise of President Obama's campaign and the impact individuals can have in changing the course of history."

—Wisconsin Senator Tammy Baldwin

❝The great potential of democracy lies in the magic people create when they decide to give of themselves for the broader public good. Here is a story of the extraordinary journey Mary Lang Sollinger experienced through choosing such a path."

—Katherine J. Cramer, author of *The Politics of Resentment: Rural Consciousness in Rural Wisconsin and the Rise of Scott Walker*

" What was going to be one became six fundraisers Mary organized for Barack Obama's Presidential campaign. She is a master organizer—energizing everyone, making it fun, making it easy, personalizing each event. I'm not sure how she did it, which is why I want you to take a look at the book. You'll learn a lot while having fun along the way."

—Dr. Zorba Paster, *National Public Radio* host of "On Your Health" and author of *The Longevity Code: Your Personal Prescription for a Longer, Sweeter Life*

" This book is a mesmerizing, personal portrait of the 2008 Obama campaign. Sollinger captures the magic of the historic campaign and Obama himself, both full of idealism and hope. She breaks barriers, just as her candidate did in 2008. This is a good read that makes a great moment in American history feel fresh and alive, contrasting them with the dark political times we live in now."

—Jo Handelsman, Director of the Wisconsin Institute for Discovery and former White House science advisor to President Barack Obama

" Mary is a true example of someone inspired to create change at the local level and, in a short time, become a major force nationally. I was happy to see the book reflected President Obama's mantra: respect, empower, include." This is a code of ethics we, in Wisconsin, understand."

—Wisconsin Congressman, Mark Pocan

" Mary and I share a deep belief in the Obama campaign mantra: respect, empower, include. By bringing people together with the belief that ordinary people can do extraordinary things for their country, Mary testifies to the better angels of our democracy. This book has a special place in my heart and is an important read for anyone who wants to help our country."

—Steven Olikara, founder and CEO, Millennial Action Project; political commentator for CNN, Fox News, NPR, and *The Washington Post,* among others.

" A campaign memoir from an actual campaign worker is rare, even though each presidential campaign gives birth to a small library of books from the higher up insiders and the reporters covering the campaign. Mary gives a look from the trenches. It is a book for students of political science that marries theory with reality."

—Tom Loftus, former Wisconsin Assembly speaker and former ambassador to Norway

" Sollinger has written a heroic and cultural work of political activism, detailing her journey from growing up in a farming community, to becoming a businessperson and becoming a delegate to the National Democratic Convention in 2008. She is reflective and truthful, both in her self-discovery and on the most serious challenges of our American Democracy."

—Dennis T. Costakos, M.D. Neonatologist

"I read how Mary Lang Sollinger started out in politics in peaceful Madison with a fundraiser, and then kept piling them on. By the time I got to this book's chapter about Indianapolis, I become a friend and indefatigable Obama supporter. Mary had a vision, and fortunately it matched Barack Obama's. Read her book."

—Edward Asner, Emmy Award-winning actor, former president of the Screen Actors Guild

"Mary Lang Sollinger is an inspiration to voters at all levels, from her neighborhood to the nation at large. Her warm and stirring book shows why: a profound commitment to living the principles of Respect, Empower, Include. The book shows how campaigning for Senator Obama changed her. The book will change you, too—and make you want to follow in her footsteps.

—Ben Wikler, Chair of the Democratic Party of Wisconsin, former Washington DC Director for MoveOn.org

"A deeply heartfelt, behind-the-scenes look at how one person can make a difference. An engrossing, personal story about how grassroots activism starts and spreads."

—Veronica Rueckert, author of *Outspoken, Why Women's Voices Get Silenced and How to Set Them Free,* and Peabody Award-winning communications specialist

"Mary has captured the essence of the formation of a candidate and campaign that changed America and the world. She exemplifies the best of what politics can bring out in us: respect, community and hope. Mary has dedicated her political life's work into funding, training and mentoring candidates, campaign staff. All she has asked in return is an open heart and mind. I implore you to take all the wisdom you can from her story and put it to action."

—John Pratt, Associate,
White House Advance Team for the President, 2012-16.

"The timing for *From Inspiration to Activism* is crucial for the upcoming elections in November. I am glad that Mary is sharing her journey and hope with us all."

—Wisconsin Congresswoman, Gwen Moore

ACKNOWLEDGMENTS

This book was made possible by those who, because of their passion for their country, stepped forward, many for the first time. Their efforts enriched those who worked with them, and their stories are recorded here to both thank and honor them for their fortitude. Many surprised themselves with what they achieved when they practiced the Golden Rule of "Do unto others as you would have them do unto you,"—the antithesis of behavior in the traditional politic world.

I would like to thank Zach Brandon, who phoned, wanting me to do a "giant" fundraiser for Senator Obama. Zach's reassuring tone made me feel that I could achieve the seemingly impossible financial goal he needed.

The evening Zach called, Heidi Wilde and Tanya Oemig were at my home and convinced me that I should do an Obama fundraiser. The next instant, they volunteered for the event. Heidi was just retired, and later on, she would be involved with more fundraisers, as well as fieldwork like knocking on doors for the Iowa primary. Her dedication helped keep me going. She always said, "Yes, I can come and help."

Many, many thanks go to Dr. Zorba Paster, who played a big role in bringing in Wisconsin for Senator Obama in both 2008 and 2012. With the popularity of his weekly radio show, he filled the rooms at many fundraisers with a cross section of people. His empathy for people made his talks sound like he was having a conversation just with you. I admired and learned so much from him.

With extended gratitude and indebtedness to Dr. Dennis and Anne Costakos, Carol Koby and her husband, Denis Carey, and Sharon Stark and spouse, Peter Livingston, whose fundraisers attracted a broad base of concerned citizens. They had relentless organizing goals, with the desire to include as many voters as possible. Also, these hosts gave me their time to meet and review their events. They took my calls when I had additional questions. They also took these fundraisers to their full potential.

In appreciation and credit to additional fundraiser hosts, including Peggy Hedberg, for twice opening up her exceptional historic home; Jan Viste and Joe and Mary Ellyn Sensenbrenner, for sharing their historic lakefront homes; and Kathy Oriel and Ellen Hartenbach, for taking time from their busy hospital schedules.

Much appreciation goes to the other headliners who made a difference for the success of this book's fundraisers. They include retired U.S. Congressman David Obey, state Assemblyman Gordon Hintz, and respected former Wisconsin Attorney General Peg Lautenschlager.

I want to acknowledge the supporters who helped make many of the events special with their time, offering ideas, making calls and presentations: Steve Busalacchi, Kathleen Falk, Governor Doyle, Wendy Skinner, Roberta Gassman, Ben and Judy Sidran, Gerri DiMaggio, Melissa Stiles, and my brother Merlin Lang.

To the many sponsors and donors. We met our goals, thanks to your generous contributions. Some donors gave at multiple events, and some brought along friends and future donors.

I offer hardy praise to Renee Knight, Bruce Green, Eric Sundquist, Neil Morris, and Joan Kozal for the hours they spent looking through their memorabilia, tracking down old emails and files for photos, and for the many phone conversations about their views of the extraordinary shared experiences we will always remember.

One group of women in a community in northern Indianapolis left an indelible mark on my heart and mind with their perceptive, kind, and straightforward guidance. I hope someday I will be able to meet them and let them know about their impact on me and how many times I shared their stories.

I want to commend Ann Muenster, John Imes, and Steve Olikara for sharing their stories of how their inspiration led to activism. After eleven years, they continue working to keep their communities involved in both issues and campaigns, as well as for bipartisanship to bring our country together.

Thank you to Ben Wikler, Felesia Martin, and J.D. Stier for their insights about "respect, empower, include," and how they incorporate these three words in their daily lives.

There were times when situations described in this book needed to be examined more deeply. Thanks to Heidi Wilde, John Odom, Georgia Berner, and Derrick Smith, who clarified, reassessed, and proofread parts of the book.

Ledell Zeller and Cindy Hoedel graciously read through the book twice before it went to the publisher. They both met deadlines. Many, many thanks for re-arranging their calendars to keep the book on schedule.

To Jay Handy who with lightening enthusiasm, sparked this book's boldness.

Many thanks go to Sandi Torkildson, who shared her wisdom on how to market and schedule book readings throughout the country from her forty years of starting, managing, and recently selling her store, A Room of One's Own, to her employees.

I am indebted to Veronica Rueckert, who made time to meet with me after the reading of her book *Outspoken*. She referred me to a friend's short list of editors in the publishing world.

At the top of the list is Dana Isaacson. I read his website thoroughly. He was a senior editor at Random House for thirteen years and is now freelancing. It took me four days to get the courage to write in a half-inch space, the allotted space for all replies. At last, I decided to take Obama's advice: "It is always about relationships and finding common ground." I found that Dana and I had an uncanny amount of common ground. He grew up in Racine, Wisconsin, and liked visiting his sister in a small town near my small town; he was a student at the University of Wisconsin–Madison, where I taught and where I live; he had worked as an intern for former Governor Tony Earl and was interested in politics.

I used half of the website space engaging us on our common ground and three sentences on the book. He emailed back and asked to see the first chapters. The rest is a result of a close and direct and professional relationship of support, encouragement, and learning to take "deep dives" into the message and goals of the book. I learned to respect the reader by staying authentic.

Since this is my first book, Dana's patience and knowledge of the industry was priceless.

Lastly, to my friends who enjoyed and experienced many campaign events and who suggested I should share them by writing a book.

To Hans, my husband, who agreed to open up our home to literally hundreds of fundraisers and events for candidates, non-profits, and our neighborhood, and still manages to say "okay" again and again. **O**

Table of Contents

CHAPTER 1

The Call

"Be sure you put your foot in the right place, and then stand firm."

—Abraham Lincoln

I first saw Barack Obama on television one afternoon in the spring of 2007. I was flipping channels and landed on the last seconds of a news segment. Onscreen I noticed a young African American man speaking to a Midwestern farm family from atop a flatbed trailer piled with hay. A number of other people had gathered behind them, also listening. The African American stepped down and greeted the farm family. The farmer pumped his hand, the farmer's wife hugged him, and their son wore a big smile.

This family was like "my people." I had grown up in Campbellsport, a small Wisconsin town of nearly a thousand people. Even though it's in the middle of the state, my friends from Madison call it "up north." This TV family's warm enthusiasm for Obama surprised me. Based on my upbringing, restraint would have been more typical from a rural family.

Yet, they were embracing a stranger, someone who didn't look like them. I thought, *What does this guy have?* I reminded myself to keep an eye out for him.

A few months later, I spotted Barack Obama's photo in *The New York Times* and read that he was the junior senator from Illinois and was running for president.

No way—the American people were not about to elect a man with a name that sounded like the world's most wanted terrorist, Osama Bin Laden. The *Times* article mentioned his book, *Dreams from My Father,* written after he'd graduated from Harvard Law School in 1991. The title suggested that Obama was fulfilling his father's dream. There was something he needed to do that his father had been unable to finish. That idea sparked my curiosity.

I was happy to find the book the next day at a locally owned bookstore. A store employee said that they had started carrying Obama's book after his electrifying speech at the 2004 National Democratic Convention. He had introduced Senator John Kerry, who won the party's nomination for president.

I read his book and thought about it for weeks afterward.

I found Obama's return to his roots interesting. A young Barry Obama had decided at some point that he wanted to be called by his more formal, first name Barack. It took courage to reclaim a distinctive name that could cause rejection. Some would question his background, but Barack had been his father's name. Obama was building a legacy.

A trip to Harvard in the late 1960s while I was a student influenced my later decision to support Barack Obama. Back then, some friends and I had planned a trip from Madison to

Boston and New York City. I was writing a term paper about starting a retail fashion business, and New York City was the mecca for clothing boutiques. I wanted to experience the retail fashion world in Manhattan. My boyfriend had graduated from Harvard and wanted to visit the Students for a Democratic Society (SDS) chapter; he was in the Madison chapter. He was curious about what their next step would be. The Harvard students had protested Secretary of Defense McNamara's proposal of escalating the war in Vietnam. SDS was an anti-Vietnam War group.

The day we were supposed to leave, his friend's car broke down. My boyfriend Bob and I had no other way to get to the East Coast. He was low on funds, and I had saved just $75 for the trip. Hitchhiking was our only option. He had hitchhiked back and forth many times from his hometown of Chicago to Harvard and had never had a problem.

It was Thanksgiving break and the weather was chilly, but he reassured me everything would be okay. In those days, hitchhiking was common. During school breaks, many university students did it to get here or there. Lots of students had great hitchhiking stories from European vacations. Except for a few friends, no one knew we were hitchhiking. Since we were already packed, a friend drove us out to the interstate.

After just three rides and sunny weather, we arrived at Harvard. It was a couple of weeks after Harvard's protest of Defense Secretary Robert McNamara's talk on campus. The secretary's car had been surrounded, and his speech stopped by the students protesting his presence. Media had covered the civil disobedience. That was the beginning of a national phenomenon and countrywide campus unrest over the Vietnam War.

That night my friend and I went to the SDS meeting in which Harvard students reviewed the McNamara protest and discussed further action. They were aware of what they had started. Columbia University was protesting now too. Madison's SDS chapter had plans in the making.

We stayed for two days. I slept at Radcliffe in the girls' dormitory. Coming from the Midwest, with basic values and a clear mindset of right and wrong, I was happy to leave. Just the week before, a young coed had jumped from the same dorm's third story and died. The way students treated each other there stood in stark contrast to how they treated each other in Madison. It was a more competitive, cut-throat atmosphere— different than what I had expected. There I learned about entitlement, privilege, and bullying.

Through the years, campuses changed and calmed down, but of course, Harvard remained competitive and one of the country's most distinguished universities. It impressed me that Barack Obama had been able to win over nearly a hundred of his fellow students and be voted the editor of the prestigious *Harvard Law Review*. Law students apply to become editors of the *Law Review* at the end of their first year and are chosen through a combination of grades and scores in a writing competition. Every year, ninety-two student-editors elect their president. The *Harvard Law Review* is the most widely cited of student law reviews. As the process goes, student Barack Obama wrote the best paper and was chosen by his fellow students to become the editor of the *Review,* the most competitive and prestigious position in all of Harvard Law School.

That was yet another reason why I supported Barack Obama early. From experiences of meeting and engaging with people later in my life, I felt that he must have developed a deep understanding and empathy for people.

One evening in late September 2007, I was at home with a small group of friends. We were creating the Madison chapter of RESULTS, an international anti-poverty advocacy group. Our meeting was interrupted by a phone call for me from Zach Brandon.

Zach was a fellow small businessperson in the University campus area. A newcomer who wanted to get involved in the community, he'd recently been recruited by me to serve on the newly formed Downtown Coordinating Committee, a stakeholder group that I chaired. Zach was smart, had great energy, and appreciated Madison's downtown. A savvy Democrat who had come to Madison from Ohio, he now ran a successful start-up business off of Madison's bustling State Street.

When Zach called that night during our meeting, he got right to the point: "Mary, I'd like you to host a fundraiser for Barack Obama."

Over the years, my husband, Hans, and I have offered up our home for a variety of Democratic and nonprofit functions. Our house faces Lake Mendota and is just a few minutes from both the city's downtown and the airport. The living room has an open balcony and is ideal for large gatherings. I had been hosting at least one Democratic and one nonprofit fundraiser every year for the past ten years.

The event that put us on the map was an October 1999 fundraiser for County Supervisor Tammy Baldwin, then running her first U.S. Congressional campaign for the House of Representatives. The night before the event, Tammy's campaign had called and asked if they could bring along Minnesota Senator Paul Wellstone, who was in town stumping for Tammy at a campus gathering. Both Tammy and Senator Wellstone had been keynote speakers for former First Lady Sue Ann Thompson's Wisconsin Women's Health Foundation annual dinner. Even though I agreed that Senator Wellstone could attend, at the time, I didn't know much about him.

Russ Feingold was listed on the invitation as our special guest. He arrived at our event with a high fever and said that he couldn't stay long. I promised that we would start the program early. When Senator Wellstone arrived, I did not recognize him and thought a stranger was crashing the event.

The program started ahead of schedule. After Russ acknowledged Tammy and her good work, he noticed the senator in the room. Russ called Wellstone up to be with him. For the next hour and a half, the two senators volleyed back and forth about their debates on the Senate floor: their wins, their disagreements, why each one was right or wrong about an issue. It was great fun to see these intelligent, high-spirited personalities feeding off each other's energy. Some of our guests took pictures of the two senators, which turned out to be priceless. For days afterward, people were talking about the Democratic "lovefest" at the Sollingers' home.

Three years later, Senator Paul Wellstone died in a plane crash. Hans and I got the news while in Arizona at a dinner for a charity bike ride event for diabetes. We had to leave the dinner due to the heartbreaking news. It was a terrible loss for the spirit of our Congress and our nation. Senator Wellstone had enjoyed friendships with fellow members in Congress on both sides of the aisle. During a national TV interview, a Republican congressman could not finish his answers about Wellstone because the senator's tragic plane accident so saddened him.

It was not unusual for me to get a call about hosting a political fundraiser, but Zach Brandon's call about Senator Barack Obama was different. "The event needs to raise a boatload of money and has to come together quickly—in just two and a half weeks." He had October 15 in mind.

"I don't know," I answered. "I'm still kind of on the fence between him and Hillary." Like so many others, I had hoped Hillary Clinton might be our first woman president. I suggested Zach call Salli Martyniak, a Madison friend who was the executive director of a nonprofit. "Salli loves Obama."

"You don't understand, Mary," Zach said. "We need a big house. And we need to bring in $140,000 that afternoon."

I wasn't sure I had heard Zach right. Then it dawned on me. "Is the candidate coming to this event?"

"Yes."

Zach had been having discussions with the Obama campaign for weeks about bringing him to Madison. Obama's staff had not been too excited about it, but Zach had been persistent. Finally, someone from the Obama team in Chicago had met with him.

The campaign worker asked Zach how much money he could raise. Zach told them they were asking the wrong question, or at least not considering the bigger picture. Sure, they could raise good money in Madison, but more importantly, bringing Obama to town would energize students at UW-Madison— exciting them enough to go to nearby Iowa and work for Obama in advance of January's critical Iowa caucuses.

Around the end of September, a couple of polls were released showing the Obama campaign in need of a lift. An ABC News/ *Washington Post* poll put him thirty-three points behind Hillary Clinton nationally. In Iowa, a *Des Moines Register* poll had him running third, though within reach—eight points behind Clinton and one point behind John Edwards. On October 2, a front-page headline in *USA Today* read: "Obama Is Still Seeking Traction." Zach's message must have resonated.

It was agreed that Candidate Obama would come to Madison for two events. He would first attend an 11 a.m. rally near campus. There would be a charge to attend, even for students, which was unusual: $15 for students, $30 for nonstudents. Following the campus event, there would be a gathering at a private home, where the cost to attend would be considerably higher at $500 per person. Obama's campaign hoped that each event could net $70,000.

Because the timeline was so tight, Zach needed an answer right away. But I wasn't sure, being still on the fence. "Hans is on a bike ride. I need to talk with him."

Zach said, "I can give you until eight o'clock tonight."

Just ninety minutes to decide. I put down the phone and explained the call to my friends at the RESULTS meeting.

They were adamant that Hans and I should host Obama. Saying it was a great opportunity, Heidi and Tanya volunteered for the event. At about 7:45, Hans finally got home from his bike ride.

At first, Hans was not enthusiastic about Zach's fundraising proposition. I said, "I've got twelve minutes to call Zach Brandon back on this." Then I added, "It's for Obama."

Hans nodded. "Okay."

The campaign set the price for the gathering at our house at $500 a person—and an additional $500 for a photo with the candidate. Those amounts were less than the campaign wanted, but Madison isn't Chicago. In Madison, that was asking for a lot of money. The date was set for Monday, October 15, from 12:45 to 2:00 p.m. at our home.

I began making calls.

Over the next few days, I phoned friends and acquaintances who were following Candidate Obama, who could pay the $500 and would want to be in the same room with him. On my first round of a dozen calls, I got few rejections. There were several yeses, a few maybes, and one or two who said, "Five hundred dollars? Mary, are you out of your mind?"

My answer was, "You will be a witness to history in the making." There was no criticism of Obama's Democratic rival Hillary.

Of the first fifteen people I contacted and pledged, seven had commitments that they could not change. I discovered that Monday was the worst day for a fundraiser. Monday is a travel day for business and vacations. Many board meetings are on Mondays, and they are often the beginning of court proceedings. To this day, I will not do a fundraiser on a Monday. Also, the scheduled time was inconvenient. It was after the lunch hour.

The toughest calls were with women friends who were also on the fence or were leaning toward supporting Hillary Clinton.

"I'd feel like a traitor," one said at the thought of not supporting the opportunity to elect a woman president. Many women felt a woman in the White House was long overdue. I understood but responded by stressing the historic nature of Obama's candidacy. I talked about how his book *Dreams from My Father* had inspired me—his charisma, brilliance, and strong sense of purpose. I had become passionate about this candidate who could heal our country after George W. Bush's disastrous second term, one in which he had taken us into the bloody and unnecessary conflict in Iraq.

I spent eight hours a day on the phone, trying to convince anyone and everyone interested that this event was a once-in-a-lifetime opportunity. For those who couldn't make it, I suggested they treat one of their family members to an early birthday or holiday present. Four people did just that.

It was coming together. Meanwhile, the original venue for the Obama on-campus event turned out to be too small for the rally—a good problem to have. The event was moved to the Orpheum Theater on State Street. After another few days, the location had to be moved yet again to the Frank Lloyd Wright designed, Monona Terrace Community and Convention Center, which could accommodate four thousand people.

Zach was right! Madison wanted to see Barack Obama.

In the week preceding Obama's Madison visit, I began hearing from his Chicago campaign staff. My principal contact was Michael O'Neil, the campaign's Midwest finance director (who eventually worked at the White House). In those calls, Michael outlined the candidate's schedule for the Madison visit, and he arranged for someone from his office to visit our home three days before the event. The Secret Service would also stop by our house and take a look. After a series of threats, Obama had received Secret Service protection early in the campaign.

Julie, the advance person from the campaign, showed up on that Friday and was delightful. She was appreciative and complimentary about our home. I had questions for her. I'd reached out to East High School and the Goodman Community Center in Madison and secured a rainbow coalition of young people to volunteer at our event: car valets, greeters, workers at the registration table, and so forth. There were adult volunteers, too, working the registration table, preparing food, and serving drinks.

I asked Julie, "Can the candidate take photos with the volunteers?" This was important to me. These hard workers had saved the campaign so much money, especially the foodies in charge of preparing all the food.

"Of course. He always takes pictures with the volunteers. They are our most important asset." That choked me up a little, further proof of Obama incorporating the value of community organizing and the idea that volunteers deserve a thank you.

On Saturday, the Secret Service arrived. They'd already told us we needed to remove the pier behind our house, having viewed it on Google Maps.

When I asked why the pier had to come out, I was told, "Don't ask, Mary." They said that more than once, always cordially but firmly.

Half a dozen agents or so walked through the house, making notes, saying they would be back the next evening for a final walkthrough. Their leader was a former Navy SEAL named Dan, polite and polished in a dark suit and sunglasses, just like in the movies.

I had friends over on Sunday to help make food for the following day's event. Though unable to pay the $500 donation, they were big fans of Obama. Learning from my mother's many parties and my friends' best recipes, we had plenty of ideas for making beautiful and delicious food for 130 donors. We created a menu Martha Stewart would be proud of. When guests later asked me who our caterer was, I was pleased to answer: "Passionate and dedicated volunteers sharing their best and most popular recipes."

On Sunday morning, my cell phone rang. The call registered "unknown number." I picked up carefully, thinking it might be a telemarketer.

"Mary, this is Barack."

I caught my breath but managed to say, "Barack, it's so nice of you to call."

"Thanks so much for hosting the fundraiser tomorrow," Obama said. "Our campaign staff is excited about coming to Madison."

I let him know how excited Madison was about meeting him and how his rally had to move to a larger venue twice.

His voice was warm, calm, and sincere. He mentioned that after our event, the campaign would be heading for California.

"In that case, I'll make a big Wisconsin basket for you and your staff to take along."

He chuckled. "That would be great."

I added, "We'll have a full house, over a hundred. I really look forward to meeting you."

On Sunday night, I made a spaghetti dinner for the fundraiser volunteers. The Secret Service did a run-through on how things would work the next day. Point man Dan brought Secret Service lapel pins for everyone, which was nice. The high school student volunteers especially liked them.

The fundraiser was tightly scheduled, beginning with Obama's arrival. He would enter our house through the garage, avoiding the front door and living room, where guests would be arriving, and enter the cleaned-out bedroom that had been turned into a photo studio. Guests would enter one by one for their photo and have a brief conversation. Some of the $1,000 donors brought their children, others a spouse, or a friend. Others brought the candidate's books *Dreams from My Father* or *The Audacity of Hope* to have signed. The program was timed for forty-three minutes: first, a welcome, which I would do, then the introduction of Wisconsin Governor Jim Doyle, who would introduce Obama. The candidate had time for three questions.

On Monday morning, the day of the fundraiser, our foodie volunteers arrived early. Across town, over four thousand people packed into Monona Terrace for Obama's 11 a.m. rally. A sociology professor from Madison's Edgewood College in the audience later told *The Capital Times*: "I was astounded by what he had to say. He rejuvenated the hope I had lost. We just haven't heard this kind of talk coming from other presidential candidates."

Toward the end of the rally, Obama's national field director, Temo took the microphone with a call to action: "We've got to do well in Iowa," he said. "It's first in the nation. It's the momentum builder. We need your help. We need your help in Iowa. We've got a lot of phone calls to make. We need to go door to door."

Michael O'Neil phoned, informing me that the Monona Terrace event had ended, and they were on their way to our house. The Secret Service had stopped by a few minutes earlier with additional precautionary security. I hadn't expected this change. It was double the number of Secret Service agents that I'd been told to expect.

"Dan, what's going on?"

"We got calls last night, Mary," he said. Dan meant threats—he didn't need to elaborate. His words burned my ears and took my breath away. This was Madison, the Tenney Lapham Neighborhood, a neighborhood where people often left their doors unlocked. We had lived here for nearly thirty years. It is one of the most liberal, safe places in the state, maybe in the whole Midwest. If Obama wasn't safe here, where could he be safe? It jarred me, and I realized what this man was risking by running for the presidency! And it was still so early in the race. He was third behind Hillary Clinton and John Edwards.

I didn't know what all these precautions entailed, but the agents kept a yellow case close at hand, next to the photo line room. Dan took me to the room and told me it contained an oxygen mask for Senator Obama in case of a gas attack. He also said, "I wish I could open up my suit jacket and show you what I have."

Sheriff Dave Mahoney later told me he got a call overnight asking him to put barricades up on our block and bring extra deputies. This reality saddened us both.

The first thing Barack Obama did when he arrived at our house was take note of the group of neighbors gathered across the street. He bounded out of his car to shake hands and talk and joke with them. One of our neighbors had the forethought to bring his video camera. He caught thirty seconds of pure joy and excitement in those gathered to see Obama.

On returning to the driveway, Obama stopped and talked to the group of Madison East High School students volunteering as valets and greeters. When he asked them questions, they looked a bit stunned. But they also appeared very happy, and some were even chatty.

Obama entered the house, and Michael O'Neil introduced Hans and me to the candidate. I welcomed him and, in my nervousness, called him Barack. I started to apologize, but he said, "Barack is fine." That set me at ease.

I led him down the hall to the room where twenty donors, some with their spouses and teenagers, stood in line for a photo. Obama was effortlessly charismatic—friendly, engaging, making jokes. We took the photos first so donors could relax and enjoy the reception without having to worry about sufficient time at the end of the event for picture taking.

After the photos, Obama signed the guests' books, some with short personal messages, when requested, on a post-it. Signing all the books seemed like a routine thing for him to do, although it was not on the schedule. Still, he sincerely did the extras. It was another "thank you" to the donors. Obama asked

Michael O'Neil, "Did we get all of them?"

As we made our way to the living room, I handed him a folder and asked if he would take a look at the proposed Senate bill inside.

When I told him it was to support micro-financing overseas, he said, "That is what my mother was doing in Jakarta." He smiled, and then I introduced Joanne Carter, the executive director from RESULTS. She had testified on behalf of this bill in U.S. Senate chambers a few days before, and this proposed piece of legislation needed his vote. She was thrilled to see how receptive he was.

Our house was full, even the upstairs balcony and the stairs in the front hall. Many guests were standing, and I could feel their excitement and anticipation. It was thrilling. I welcomed and thanked the 130 guests for coming. Usually, I would have been nervous, but I felt like this was the right place to be. I introduced Democratic Governor James Doyle. He had not formally endorsed Obama but would a short time later.

I could see the Secret Service agents getting restless as Doyle's speech went on a bit long. They wanted to stay on schedule. Still, the governor was exceptional, comparing Barack Obama to John F. Kennedy. I thought such a stellar speech might put pressure on Obama, but of course, it didn't.

Candidate Barack Obama was outstanding—relaxed and funny but also serious and passionate. He shouted hellos to Madison attorneys Chuck Barnhill and Bill Dixon. Obama had worked in the Chicago office of Miner, Barnhill, and Galland—a law firm with public interest and social justice priorities. Their Madison office included Chuck and Bill.

Obama mentioned that he'd traveled to the Madison law office on several occasions and had also come to socialize and spent time at the Memorial Union Terrace. He pointed out our living room window and across Lake Mendota toward the University of Wisconsin's student union. He said that while he was single, he'd had some dates there. "Don't tell Michelle," he joked.

Why was he so relaxed and positive? I'm sure part of it was that he'd just had a strong, successful rally, with more people than anyone expected. You could tell that this candidate liked and enjoyed people. He felt comfortable with them and they with him. He was relaxed and upbeat even though just a few days before some discouraging poll numbers were released. They had him twenty points behind Hillary Clinton in Iowa and even more so nationally.

I learned later in *Game Change*, the book on the 2008 campaign by John Heilemann and Mark Halperin, that shortly after those polls were released, Obama met with his most trusted advisors in a conference room in downtown Chicago. They were not gaining momentum. It was decided that Obama had to engage in a spirited debate with Hillary Clinton to decide who was the best Democratic candidate to deliver the change voters so clearly wanted. Obama had kept his opponents at arm's length. According to *Game Change*, Obama told his advisors that he would engage and debate Clinton, but he would have nothing to do with anything close to a smear campaign. Many of the political debates in the past had devolved into dueling matches, displaying which candidate could deliver the hardest punches. That was not Obama's style, and he wasn't going to conform to the status quo. He practiced what he preached and what he believed in.

"If I ever catch anyone digging into the Clintons' personal lives," he said, "you will be fired."

He left that meeting feeling energized, ready for a debate. "We're going to win this," he said.

That was the Obama we saw on October 15 in Madison.

A few days before the event, I had asked the advance people if Obama would take questions at our event. I hoped he would. People who were paying that kind of money should be able to ask the candidate a question.

"We always take questions."

Madison restaurateur Chris Berge asked about Obama's views on African policy, and Obama gave an insightful response. Milele Chikasa Anana, the publisher of *UMOJA*, a magazine for Madison's African American community, asked a question about minorities and education. I don't remember Obama's response, but she did not like his answer. I suppose as an African American woman who had some years on the candidate, she felt she had the right to say so.

"That's not good enough," Milele said.

I was mortified. Would this be an embarrassing or, worse yet, a defeating moment for Obama?

As a former mayoral candidate, I knew to give a wrong or unacceptable answer could take a candidate out of favor with the group. There was no air in the room. You could hear a pin drop. I was counting the seconds, *one Mississippi, two Mississippi*, as nine seconds passed. That was a long time standing there in front of over a hundred voters.

Barack lifted the microphone, looked her straight in the eye, and gave his second answer.

"Humph. Much better!" Milele said. What a relief! I could start breathing again. Milele's question was the last one.

When he handed me the microphone, I pointed out the Wisconsin cheese and chocolate basket we had for his staff for their flight to California. I thanked our guests again for joining us and supporting Senator Obama. I turned off the microphone and thanked him for his engaging talk and for taking questions.

Many of the guests rushed him. It was a bit of a scramble, with people wanting to get close to Candidate Obama, asking more questions and taking selfies. I saw that security was trying to steer him toward the garage door.

At one point, I panicked when I lost sight of him. I asked Dan, "Where's the senator?"

"In the garage," Dan said, "taking photos with volunteers."

Even though he was behind schedule, Obama and his staff kept their word and took time for pictures with the volunteers. At the moment, volunteers were more important than the schedule. All the volunteers were so grateful and happily engaged while talking with Obama. To this day, I spot pictures of that event in volunteers' offices and homes. When I point out the framed picture, they beam, and we take a few minutes to reminisce.

The Obama group departed soon after, but none of the guests were in a hurry to leave. They'd just witnessed something special. It felt like we had been a part of history. People were milling around, smiling, laughing, some with tears in their eyes. When people were finally leaving, many asked about doing more—volunteering or writing another check. I heard, "He has to be our next president," and "What can I do to help him win the nomination?"

I answered, "Let's go to Iowa. I will give you a call," which I did.

I was happy. The event had surpassed the $70,000 goal, but it was more than that. I felt that the world could be changed, that our country would be better if Obama could be the president. He was the one who could do it. My husband, Hans, who is not easily impressed, said to me, "Mary, we've got to stay with this guy."

We did.

For weeks after Obama's visit to Madison, people were talking about the huge rally at Monona Terrace. Guests from our event were sharing their signed Obama books at their homes and offices. The photo line and volunteers' pictures were arriving at their homes in the mail from the campaign, along with thank you notes. Many shared their selfies, photos, and pictures of their signed books on Facebook. The Obama buzz continued unabated.

The morning after our fundraiser, I received a call on my cell phone. Again, it said "unknown number."

It was Barack Obama thanking me for the wonderful event. I asked him if there was enough food in the Wisconsin basket for everyone, and I heard the smile in his voice when he answered, "Yes." He said he was in San Francisco and had another fundraiser in a few hours. I wished him well and told him I appreciated his call. It would be six months before I would have a one on one conversation with him again. O

CHAPTER 2

The December Call-a-Thon

"Leave nothing for tomorrow that can be done today."

—Abraham Lincoln

Zach Brandon phoned again in early December 2007. He wanted me to organize a call-a-thon to raise funds for Candidate Obama in the Iowa primary. Zach said Obama's poll numbers were slowly rising, although Hillary Clinton continued to have a strong lead, and John Edwards remained in second place.

Zach convinced me that my house was the ideal venue. He wanted to put volunteers in each room to make calls. Due to the upcoming holidays and the UW students taking their end of the semester exams, there was again a narrow time frame.

We would arrange car rides for students to our house. The University campus is a forty-minute walk, so car rides were essential to save time in the frigid weather.

Working with Zach and Bryon Eagon, the University of Wisconsin's student lead organizer for Obama for America, we combined our lists. Zach had a list from the campaign headquarters. All three of us had been collecting names of Obama supporters. Since Facebook was just catching on, many of our lists were built on word of mouth. Of course, I included the list of donors from the October 15 fundraiser.

We organized a three-evening call-a-thon. I made homemade chicken soup for the volunteers. There were about twenty-five of them, less than expected from our three volunteer lists, but that didn't deter our energy. We just stayed on the phones longer.

There was an incentive for the donors we were calling. The volunteers had received a list of what each donation could "buy." For instance, if someone made a $500 donation, that would buy a TV ad during *Oprah* in Des Moines and Cedar Rapids. These were fun talking points that everyone could relate to.

December is not ordinarily a good month for fundraising, and we were a bit disappointed. We had been hoping to accomplish more. We ended up raising $5,500 for the Obama Iowa primary campaign. But we rationalized that if Wisconsin, a small state with approximately 990,000 Democrats, could do $5,500, multiplying this sum by fifty states would yield $275,000 for the Iowa primary. We felt better.

As a thank you for Zach, Bryon, and my organizing efforts, we were included on a Midwest conference call with Candidate Barack Obama and Iowa State Director Paul Tewes. There would be time for five or six questions from the organizers who were on the phone. These questions focused on the polls that were going up in Obama's favor. It was a thrill to hear Candidate Obama's voice thanking us for our calls, especially during the holidays. I could hear his confidence and optimism. I felt empowered at being part of a big plan to make a difference for our country.

Again, the Madison volunteers asked what more they could do.

We sent out an email asking for sign-ups to get out the vote (GOTV) for the Iowa primary on January 3, 2008. That meant door-to-door canvassing.

Being from Wisconsin, I knew how cold the windy farm fields and small towns could be while knocking on doors. We wondered who would be in Madison and be available. How many would head down to Iowa in the middle of winter?

For me, that October 15 fundraiser had been the result of my longtime community organizing projects and from running retail stores on State Street on the University of Wisconsin campus. The October event put me as the go-to person for further information regarding Candidate Obama.

I had compiled a list of nearly two hundred names from the October 15 fundraiser and the call-a-thon. At the end of each emailed invitation, it said, "Please share this invitation with anyone you think would be interested." Also, I had my cell phone on all my emails. These two small things made it easy to connect with me and for the supporter to be notified of future events and other fundraisers for Barack.

After the presidential election of November 4, 2008, the Obama list had over four hundred active and responsive contacts in the Madison area. Following Barack Obama's inauguration in January 2009, I thought my work was done. I sent out an email asking who wanted to be taken off the Obama list. I was moving on and had just accepted the full-time position of finance director for the Democratic Party of Wisconsin. Much to my surprise, I had supporters call or email back concerned that the emails would be ending. They wanted to be kept informed. They wanted to stay connected to President Obama and First Lady Michelle Obama.

As it turned out, during the off-election years of 2009 to 2010, the list came in handy. There were additional events: The Democratic National Convention, White House opportunities, and a few visits from high-profile national Democratic leaders to Madison for fundraisers.

The list remains active with over seven hundred names. Over the last eleven years, there have been only a handful of requests asking to be removed from it, mainly because the person was moving out of state. **O**

CHAPTER 3

The First Door is the Hardest

"The role of a citizen in a Democracy does not end with your vote."

—Barack Obama

Dubuque may not be widely considered a desirable destination during the snowy month of December, but we still had a good response from sturdy Wisconsin Badgers when we sent out an email asking who was up for going to Iowa for the primary and working for Senator Obama. Many volunteers had already been receiving emails from the Obama campaign and were organizing groups and making driving plans. Some made arrangements to stay with family and friends.

With eight days remaining before the state primary on January 3, 2008, we made our first trip to Iowa with three cars of volunteers. Since many in our group had just one day to volunteer, I requested that we work in the Dubuque area. We would be knocking on doors, handing out literature, and doing whatever else was asked of us to support Barack Obama.

In downtown Dubuque, all of the presidential candidates had offices in storefront buildings: Hillary Clinton, John Edwards, Bill Richardson, Joe Biden, Christopher Dodd, Mike Gravel, and Dennis Kucinich. This was Iowa, where presidential dreams launch or turn to dust.

The Obama headquarters was a big room with a table full of food and a large wall covered top to bottom with notes. I went to the wall and read heartfelt and energizing messages of thanks and best wishes from across the country. These seemed to signal that Obama's community organizing background was making a difference. Everybody counts, everybody can make a difference, and everyone can participate. The display gave the room energy. Below the opposite wall, at more than a dozen desks, volunteers worked at computers.

A volunteer greeted our group of Madisonians, encouraging us to get something to eat. A few minutes later, a middle-aged campaign staffer provided campaign materials for knocking on doors. Because we had cars, we would be driving to a small town, about thirty minutes west.

She reviewed the materials on clipboards, which included names and addresses of people who, in the past, had voted Democratic. Our sheets had a listing of the names, addresses, ages, and genders of those who were to be contacted. We would mark our sheets with an "x" at NH (not home), NA (no access), or M (moved). The last question was difficult because it asked who they intended to vote for, and many people felt this question was too personal. Their answers could be unpredictable.

The maps of the neighborhoods looked well organized and made sense. Some stops were at farms on the way to the small town. If no one was home, we would leave Obama brochures. We were instructed to be polite and gracious, to listen to people and their concerns, and to write them down. This whole process was called canvassing or getting out the vote.

As we were reviewing the information, a young energized man came over to our group, smiling. "How are you doing, Wisconsin?" It was Michael Dorsey, the Midwest political director for the Obama campaign. He told us where we would be canvassing and laid out the ground rules: go in groups of two, never go inside a house, and make sure you stay warm. They gave us cellophane packaged hand warmers for the inside of our gloves. Michael also told us to take food along.

He ended by saying, "While canvassing for the campaign, you are acting as a representative of Senator Obama. At all times, we must remain respectful, polite, and kind to the people we encounter."

We started on our way, but before we reached the door, Mike called out, "Wait a minute. Come back! I forgot to tell you about REI."

Given my retail background, I thought he had something for us from REI—the outdoor retailer Recreational Equipment, Inc. I thought we might be getting a fleece scarf with the wonderful Obama campaign logo of the rising sun.

Mike meant something else entirely. He said, "REI stands for respect, empower, and include. Remember those three words when you are knocking on doors."

That struck a powerful chord within me. The campaign's respectful and welcoming culture and Obama's resistance to the conventional modern political campaign strategy that requires trying to destroy the opposition was summed up in those three letters and the words they represented. I knew I was working for the right candidate. I was empowered. This was the first time I had ever knocked on the doors of strangers' homes. What would they say?

The first door was the hardest.

Iowans were accustomed to their state being the first in the nation with a presidential primary or caucus. Most were good-spirited and listened to our pitch. Some were tired but still polite upon seeing yet another volunteer for another candidate at their door. They seemed to respect that we were out working for Obama in single-digit weather. We were sincere and minded our manners. A few commented that the Obama volunteers stood out as being exceptionally respectful.

After that first day, we returned to Madison after the sun went down, and the weather turned even more frigid. We had a lot to talk about and felt like we had made a difference. All of us had been impressed by the hospitality of the Obama office. It seemed like no one there had a private or self-serving agenda. We felt appreciated. We shared the common goal of working for our country and for Senator Obama.

On the next Iowa trip, I stayed overnight, sleeping on a cot in a private residence in a small town outside of Dubuque. There were a number of people from other parts of the Midwest being put up at this same home, all of us arriving at different times.

In the morning, our hostess prepared a wonderful farmer's breakfast for us. The chatter over this delicious breakfast was inspirational. One volunteer was from the East Coast. I was impressed she had traveled so far. This was a great way to start a long day in the cold weather.

On the day of the primary, three volunteers made the drive with me from Wisconsin to Iowa. Heidi Wilde was a retired University of Wisconsin administrator. She was from Germany and had emigrated to America. She cared about her adopted country and the opportunities it gave her (see Chapter 10). My daughter Muffy also joined the group, taking time from her winter college break. Also with us was another college student who had connected with us through the campaign's website. We didn't know him, but we were happy to take another volunteer to Dubuque for Obama.

It was a typical cold Midwestern winter day with temperatures in the single digits. I occupied my time by knocking on doors in Dubuque. Heidi and Muffy held up large signs at busy intersections over the afternoon and rush hour. The college student disappeared with another group.

The Obama campaign had a great system of connecting volunteers with each other. I assumed it was all on software designed to organize and send volunteers efficiently to the towns they had signed up for. Maybe Chris Hughes, the Harvard roommate who was the co-founder with Mark Zuckerberg for Facebook, had created the software. He was the originator of many of the campaign's tech programs, which collected over two million volunteer profiles by the campaign's end.

Late in the afternoon, we returned to the Dubuque office for our caucus assignments and then headed to a high school gym to see Senator Obama and Michelle. After traveling the state, they had stopped in Dubuque. It was thrilling to see both Obamas at a relatively small rally of approximately four hundred supporters of all ages. They both spoke about hope and change, thanking everyone for our work in the field while including endearing comments about knocking on doors in beastly cold winter weather. Senator Obama's speech ended with "Yes, we can!" The gym filled with energy and optimism.

After the rally, we drove to the school where that Iowa precinct's caucus was being held. When we got out of the car in the parking lot, it was nasty cold. The weather was frigid, with a wind chill below zero. There were a good number of cars already there. It was amazing to see so many civic-minded people heading into the school. Quite a few had young children with them.

Each of the candidates had meeting rooms, but only the Obama campaign had sectioned off a room for babysitting so delegates could drop off their kids. This idea had empowered more caucus members to attend. Michael Dorsey and Obama's campaign staff had expected a large turnout, and they were right.

Someone on the campaign told me, "Mary, we need you and Muffy to babysit in the kids' room." Much of my time at the Iowa caucuses was spent wiping noses and prepping baby bottles. That was fine with Muffy and me. Our attitude was, "Wherever you need us."

Wisconsin doesn't have a caucus system, so it was my first time witnessing this event. The energy was incredible. There was particularly a lot of excitement in Candidate Obama's part of the hall. As the evening progressed, delegates were being persuaded to consolidate to their next favorite candidate. The Obama and Hillary areas had about the same number of people. John Edwards' part of the room was shrinking substantially.

Later, I couldn't resist and left the babysitting room for a few minutes to see what was happening in the caucus room. Just two candidates' signs were left: Senators Obama and Clinton. About an hour later, a parent came in to pick up his kids.

I asked if the caucus was finished.

"Almost."

Then all at once, many more parents joyously arrived. Candidate Obama had won this precinct caucus. Could it be possible that he might win all of Iowa?

We returned to our freezing cars, relieved when their engines started up. We would be gathering at a sports bar down the street from the Dubuque headquarters for the announcement of the winner of all the state caucuses. Soon after our arrival, Michael Dorsey shared the results. Seconds later, it was on the large TV screen.

Barack Obama had won Iowa with 37.6 percent of the vote—a strong nine percentage points ahead of John Edwards and Hillary Clinton! Over 200,000 Democratic votes were counted that night, compared to 124,000 in 2004. What a spectacular and stunning win! There were tears of joy at the bar.

As Heidi, Muffy, and I drove back to Madison, we still couldn't quite believe it. We discussed our experiences and what this could mean for the next primary in New Hampshire. It hit us that we had just witnessed a part of history.

Halfway back to Madison, I got a call from a friend, a strong Hillary supporter who had been at a caucus precinct in Des Moines. As one of my friends who couldn't believe I was supporting Obama and not Hillary Clinton, she was now venting about the Iowa caucus results. She had not been talking to me in the past months.

"The freaking guy had babysitting rooms!" she said.

"I know. I was in one of those rooms."

"What were you doing babysitting?"

"It didn't matter what I was doing. Doing anything to help Obama win was the issue." That was followed by a few expletives from her.

Despite my friend's frustrations, the ride went fast. We knew that this was just the beginning. The campaign volunteers had dedication, passion, and no personal agendas. They were working for the bigger picture—for the love of our country. Everyone was walking the talk of respect, empower, and include.

Years later, as the 2012 elections approached, Outagamie County Executive Tom Nelson was testing the waters for a run at a statewide office. He left me a voicemail seeking support.

When I returned his call, he answered on his cell. He was walking the streets, knocking on doors to meet more voters. It was a late January afternoon, the sun was setting, and it was nearly zero degrees in the Appleton area—typical weather for that time of year. Instead of calling it a day, Tom said that he had one more block to do and would call me back.

I wanted to support someone who had state legislative experience, enthusiasm, and work ethic. After we talked, I knew Tom fit the bill.

I also inquired if Tom knew of a strong Obama volunteer in his area, someone with whom I could coordinate for the 2012 election. That's how I hooked up with the wonderful Ann Muenster. She was well-known as an organizer in the 2008 Organizing for America presidential campaign. Tom gave me Ann's contact information.

When I phoned her a few days later, Ann described her volunteer work in 2008 and the support she was building for the upcoming 2012 November election. I was thrilled to speak with her. My goal was to connect Obama supporters in her area to Obama campaign events, fundraisers, and announcements I would receive because of my role of being on Obama's National Finance Campaign Committee. I asked Ann if she would be my connector for the Fox Valley, a large area on the northeastern side of the state. Before 2008, that area voted Republican. Tom felt that Ann's volunteer work and organizing efforts had a lot to do with it going for Senator Obama in the November, 2008 presidential election.

I clarified what I was asking: it was mainly forwarding my campaign emails to her, and she would then forward them to her lists. She agreed.

Ann's inspiring story on the Obama campaign trail was similar to that of so many other field organizers and volunteers I met when canvassing and knocking on doors. She had grown up in a family where her grandmother religiously watched *Meet the Press* every Sunday morning. As a diesel truck mechanic, her dad's daily ritual included reading the Madison *Capital Times* as soon as he got home from work. The family dinner table normally had political discussions, and Ann's parents routinely took her along as they voted in every election.

There was a joy she felt as a child by being given the responsibility of pulling the red lever that drew the curtain shut on the voting booth. It set her on a course of voting, but her engagement in the campaign process would not happen until she was fifty-five years old.

Although Ann attended campaign rallies when presidential candidates visited Madison and Appleton, she felt no need to volunteer or get involved in a political campaign, other than voting on Election Day.

That changed February 10, 2007, when Senator Barack Obama announced his candidacy for president. Like so many other people, Ann had been awed by his speech at the Democratic National Convention in 2004 and had a sense of his greatness. When she read his second book, *The Audacity of Hope,* Ann found that she shared the same values and the same hope for our country, as did Senator Obama.

She believed that we could find common ground among people if we only took the time to listen and understand each other's perspectives. After reading Obama's book, she knew that if he decided to run for president, she would find a way to play a role in his campaign.

Senator Barack Obama announced his candidacy on February 10, 2007, on the steps of the Illinois State Capitol. Taking the step to get involved in President Obama's campaign involved the simple act of saying, "Yes."

It was the same for Ann. For her, it happened on June 12, a sunny day in June outside Kaukauna High School in Kaukauna, Wisconsin. Ann was eagerly waiting in line behind hundreds of people, all of them wanting a ticket for the next day's town hall meeting with Senator Obama. Fortunately, she was available because a week earlier, school had still been in session, and she would have had to be in the classroom with her students.

When at long last, Ann was in front of the table with the campaign workers, she asked, "Do you need any more volunteers?" Yes, they did. At that moment, a door opened. It would change her life.

Ann returned that night to receive directions for the town hall meeting. She helped set up chairs in the gymnasium, and the next day she directed people to their designated area. She hoped to meet Senator Barack Obama. Ann didn't hesitate to ask a campaign worker if she might have her book signed if she brought it the next day. Surprisingly, the worker encouraged her and other volunteers to do just that.

Assisting with the town hall was quite a thrill for Ann, as well as working with young campaign workers from different parts of the country who were traveling as Senator Obama's advance team. Their dedication to the campaign and their exuberance were infectious.

The Kaukauna town hall meeting was the first time she saw President Obama in person, and she was incredibly impressed by his authenticity as he sat down with a local couple and talked *with*—not at—Ryan and Jenny about the economic struggles they were facing. It all went by way too fast.

Active campaigning for Candidate Obama began July 19, 2008, the day the campaign office opened in Appleton. Supporters crowded into the small office to hear what needed to be done. The field organizers mostly needed people to knock on doors and listen to voters, but Ann was nervous about doing that.

Still, she was determined to play a part in bringing about change to our country. When the votes would be counted on November 4, and we would learn who would be our next president, Ann wanted to be sure that if Obama lost, she would not be lamenting, "I should have helped." And if he won, she would be able to say, "I helped elect President Obama."

Over the next four months, Ann came to the campaign office two to three times a week. Every time she arrived, she was warmly greeted by one of Obama's young and earnest staff field organizers.

Bob, Andrew, and Richard embraced the Obama culture of respect, empower, and include. They had a clear sense of shared purpose that allowed them to set their egos aside. They treated each other and each volunteer with respect. It didn't matter to them that so many were new to campaigning. Their patience and interest in helping every volunteer gain confidence empowered everyone involved to persevere.

Ann became frustrated when asked to use an automatic telephone number dialer to efficiently reach voters during the GOTV efforts. She was having a difficult time getting in sync with the automatic pick-up and exactly when she needed to start talking. This was new technology in 2008, and the process unnerved Ann. She was about to give up and ask Andrew for a paper list, or else she thought she might go home or ask for a different task. But Andrew took the time to sit down and work with her until she got the hang of it. That was empowering for Ann.

The memory of that moment inspires her still today to support other volunteers with the same respect she was shown. She is certain that if there is a conscious decision to respect, empower, and include people, they are capable of so much more.

Canvassing voters is another activity many volunteers are nervous to initiate. Partnering with another volunteer seemed to be the answer. Luckily, Ann met Janice Morton at the office. They hit it off. They were kindred spirits.

Janice had recently retired after working for Waupaca and Outagamie Counties as a social worker, and Ann had one more year left to teach in the Appleton Area School District as a speech and language pathologist. They were in professions where listening and collaboration were important skills, and they were ready to put them to use.

From August to Election Day, Janice and Ann went canvassing together. Midweek, one of them would call the other to inquire about their plans for the weekend. Would they canvass Saturday or Sunday? Which shift worked best? They figured it out every weekend, met at the office, picked a territory (or turf), and set out. Each of them carried a clipboard with their walk sheets split between them. One took the odd side of the street, while the other took the even.

They stayed in view of each other. If Janice was lingering at a voter's door, Ann joined her on the stoop, hanging back to allow Janice to lead the conversation, but if it felt right, Ann would add her voice. Janice did the same for her. They had each other's back.

Ann was an ordinary person doing something extraordinary. The proof would come on November 4, 2008. One voter at a time, she listened to their stories of losing their job, their healthcare stories, and their cynicism about the political process. She sought to build connections and trust, hoping they would recognize that she cared about their concerns, as Obama did. As his ambassador, Ann felt a personal responsibility. So many times, Ann felt skepticism give way to hope, which energized her to continue.

A turning point was Octoberfest, an annual festival in downtown Appleton. College Avenue, the Wisconsin town's main street, was lined with the booths of nonprofit organizations selling food. While most in attendance focused on eating their way down the street, people that year were also paying close attention to the campaign. The Democratic Party of Outagamie County had a booth that attracted a lot of attention, but when it was discovered that there were no Obama yard signs there or inside the campaign office, folks got irritated. There was a shortage of yard signs provided by the Obama campaign, and no one at the festival knew when orders might be filled.

Ann understood supporters' frustration as the would-be Democratic voters saw scads of McCain yard signs leaving with Octoberfest festivalgoers. She answered their outrage by slipping into the campaign office a few blocks away to discuss it with one of the field organizers. Without knowing where to order signs locally or what they might cost, Ann left the campaign office with a yellow legal pad and pen in hand and returned to the county party booth.

She called out to anyone within earshot that if they were interested in having an Obama yard sign, they could sign up for one. "Leave your name and phone number," she instructed. Later, she left with three pages of names.

After checking with a local candidate, Ann and her husband called a printer and started by ordering two hundred signs. As soon as they were ready, they picked them up from the printer in Fond Du Lac, who was thirty-three miles away. They stapled them onto the wires and delivered them to the campaign office and then began calling the list of supporters from Octoberfest. To cover the cost, supporters left a $2 donation per sign. By the campaign's end, eight hundred signs had been ordered and paid for—a win-win.

The way the field organizers handled her independent ordering of yard signs was another example of the culture of respect within the Obama campaign. While Ann ordered signs outside the parameters of the official campaign, the field organizers recognized that it was important to include volunteers in the decision-making and empower them to take initiatives, as long as our efforts were consistent with the shared purpose of electing Barack Obama. Volunteers were trusted and felt more committed to the campaign.

Ann's free time on the weekends was used to campaign, while weekdays were filled with teaching and using the 2008 election as a teachable moment in history. Most of her students needed support in developing their receptive and expressive language.

Strengthening the word-meaning relationships supported their academic progress, so Ann set out to use the election as a means for teaching vocabulary, analogous relationships, and more, all while remaining nonpartisan.

Beyond the presidential election, the picture book *Vote!* by Eileen Christelow provided excellent content for a number of her students' teaching objectives while introducing them to civics education.

On her own time, Ann readily shared her preference for Barack Obama with her colleagues, so it was no surprise to anyone when she took a personal day on November 4, 2008, so that she could get out the vote on Election Day.

Janice and Ann teamed up for the last time, checking out two turfs to remind supporters to vote and offer literature explaining where their polls were located. When knocking on doors, if they found people at home, they asked if they had voted yet. If not, when were they planning to go? Janice and Ann worked to reach every voter.

They even took advantage of an unseasonably warm day to enjoy lunch outside overlooking the Fox River from a local restaurant. All their work over the last four months would soon be over, and it felt right to take time to enjoy the friendship that had developed between them.

Mostly through emails, Ann and I continue to work together, though once or twice a year, we would see each other at a statewide party event and have a good talk. Talking with her is always like talking to an old friend.

Ann's experience on the campaign was like so many of the stories shared by hundreds of thousands of ordinary Americans stirred by President Obama's message. With Obama, we were fortunate to have an inspirational candidate.

President Obama left us a legacy about how to organize and how to practice respect, empower, include—all based on the age-old Golden Rule. Time after time, we saw his dedication to the people of this country. He practiced a truly democratic process of "We, the people."

The power to create change lies within each of us. **O**

CHAPTER 4

A Turn-key Fundraiser

"Fired up! Ready to Go."
—Edith Childs, Greenwood, SC

When Hillary Clinton won New Hampshire on January 8, 2008, everything turned upside down. But we Obama supporters were far from discouraged. I was working to organize a second Madison Obama fundraiser, and my friend Peggy Hedberg asked me to organize an event for February 5. She had been at my October fundraiser and called a few weeks later, wanting to do something for Obama. I was thrilled, of course, and we met to organize the event. Peggy has a beautiful historic home in Maple Bluff, just two doors from our governor's executive residence. Governor Doyle would be the special guest and headliner at Peggy's event.

Peggy was well known for her preservation efforts. Some time ago, her historic house caught fire in the middle of the night, and the fire wasn't detected until substantial damage had already occurred. Her restoration efforts were written up a number of times in our newspapers. She had been applauded by the community's strong historic preservation supporters.

Peggy gave me phone numbers of her Maple Bluff friends and neighbors who she knew were interested in Candidate Obama. For making calls, I also accessed my growing October 15 fundraiser list.

Peggy graciously supplied a caterer for the wine and beverages, saving the campaign over $1,000. All donations that night would go to the campaign. There were no expenses. I started calling these "turn-key fundraisers" because the campaign didn't have to use any of their funds or their staff time. I always felt that the staff appreciated this effort to make their jobs less stressful and their financial goals a bit easier to achieve. These fundraisers for our statewide candidates were much appreciated because the campaign staff would just come to the event with the candidate. It saved the understaffed statewide campaigns substantial time and work.

We had a full house. During the fundraiser, I received a call from Michael O'Neil, my contact person and Obama's Midwest finance director, asking if I had heard from Penny Pritzker, the campaign's national finance chairwoman. At that time, I didn't know who she was. They wanted me to be on Obama's National Finance Committee.

That was a new world for me. I didn't know what a national finance committee did. I told Mike I hadn't heard from Penny. Besides, I couldn't talk right now. I was at a fundraiser, and the governor was due to arrive in a few minutes, and I needed to brief him about his speech for the program. I would call him back the next morning. He seemed a bit surprised but agreed.

Governor Doyle had formally endorsed Senator Obama in January. This fundraiser gave the governor a platform to share his reasons for endorsing the senator this early, and he again referred to Senator Obama as a young John F. Kennedy, saying he could inspire many and had a vision of change for our country.

That night, I also was determined to meet Dr. Zorba Paster. Zorba was a Madison physician and is well-known across the state for his long-running Saturday morning show on *Wisconsin Public Radio*. I had spotted his name as one of the fundraiser's sponsors and was hoping that he would be attending.

I didn't know Zorba. I wasn't even sure what he looked like. When I asked someone at Peggy's event if he was there, I was pointed to the kitchen, where I found Zorba with other guests. I waited until some left the conversation, then introduced myself. In a quiet corner of the kitchen, I asked if he would consider being the headliner at an event in Waupaca for Candidate Obama's campaign. The Waupaca County Democrats would organize it, and we would work around Zorba's schedule. The chair of that local group, Jon Baltmanis, was a kidney transplant patient. He had tracked me down from a Milwaukee newspaper article. Jon had recognized my last name, as my husband, Hans, had performed his kidney transplant.

Jon got my email address and wrote me a long, passionate plea to have Candidate Obama come to his town of Weyauwega. It took over fifteen minutes to read. While I had found it impossible to say no, I replied with, "Let's see what I can make happen."

My brother Merlin had lived in Waupaca for thirty years. It was ten miles away from Weyauwega. Many times, he spoke to me of listening to *Wisconsin Public Radio* and how popular the shows were in his area. He had mentioned that Dr. Zorba was incredibly popular. That had opened the door for me to listen to WPR, and I, too, became a faithful listener. Dr. Zorba's show was one of my favorites. When Jon's heartfelt email arrived, I had already been a longtime fan of WPR and Zorba.

After I told Zorba Jon's story, he said, "It sounds kind of interesting, and Obama's campaign is something I should be involved with." His open-mindedness and acceptance were great news. But first, Zorba had to check with *Wisconsin Public Radio* and their contract. He would get back to me in a day or two.

His reply gave me the confidence to call Jon with an update. I made the call from Peggy's basement steps. After I told him, I thought Jon was going to jump right through my cell phone. I had to repeat that there was only a fifty-fifty chance this would work out. I'd keep him in the loop.

I called back Michael O'Neil the next day. He explained what Senator Obama's National Finance Committee (NFC) was. It was a periodic gathering of all the major Obama fundraisers in the country. Many of these people had wealthy friends who would write checks when asked. Others did receptions with the candidate, while others did events with surrogates—famous people who could draw a crowd and who also supported Obama. Michael excitedly invited me to the March meeting, but we had a family ski vacation planned on the dates, and I was not able to cancel it.

He seemed frustrated and said how important it was for me to be there. I apologized and said that I needed to spend time with my family. I had done six fundraisers in seven months for our candidate, working five to six days a week.

He thanked me and said some kind words. Then he told me the date for the next NFC meeting in early May in Indianapolis. I was free and put it on my calendar. Supporters from all over the country would be meeting. Michael said he'd get back to me with more details in two or three weeks.

I was glad the meeting would be relatively close. I would drive and knew the route well; Muffy, my daughter, had gone to the University of Indiana for four years.

Zorba called the following day. He said that he was in his office with patients, so our conversation was short. "*Wisconsin Public Radio* said it was okay. Since I would be representing myself, there is no conflict of interest."

"Many thanks, Zorba. You made my day. Jon will be thrilled."

In the next few months, he only had February 14, Valentine's Day, available.

His wife, Penny, would be attending the event too. Thank goodness she was an Obama supporter too. **O**

CHAPTER 5

The Humble and Inspiring Fundraiser in the Heartland

"And in the end, it is not the years in your life, it's the life in your years."

—Abraham Lincoln

An intense guy and active in politics, Jon Baltmanis was the Democratic chair for Waupaca County. He was proud of his Lithuanian heritage and said that was the reason he had survived so many health issues related to childhood diabetes. He was legally blind, but that didn't stop him. Ecstatic to hear Zorba's good news, Jon had a plan ready to go.

Located in central Wisconsin, Weyauwega was a small town of just over a thousand people. For such a small town, with tough logistics with transportation, I didn't want to call up Michael for a surrogate or headliner from the campaign. I knew the amount of donations generated for the event would be low compared to regular fundraisers.

But l also didn't want to disappoint Jon. For the locals, Dr. Zorba was neutral; he wasn't a politician. He could be trusted and knew how to talk to the people in northern Wisconsin, and he was willing. Perhaps Zorba had even more draw than a Democratic politician. Waupaca was known to be more "red" than "blue."

I connected Jon with my brother Merlin. Since nearby Waupaca was a larger town of nearly six thousand, it would be accessible for more people. Jon agreed. The next day, with Merlin's help, a campaign event with Dr. Zorba was scheduled at Bon Marche, a popular combination diner-bookstore on Main Street. Owner Bonnie was very excited to have Dr. Zorba and the Obama fundraiser at her business. Seven at night worked well for her. Jon and Merlin thought $35 per person would be good.

Jon was working through his email list of county Democrats, and he and his wife were making phone calls to homes, mostly on landlines. Merlin was also talking up the event with his friends at his daily 6 a.m. coffee at the truck stop, as well as at church. He made calls to friends he thought would be interested. Bonnie put up a sign at the Bon Marche and talked up the event to staff and customers. Since Dr. Zorba was representing himself, the public radio station was not legally permitted to announce the event.

My brother is a pretty mellow guy, but seeing Merlin getting excited about meeting Dr. Zorba, you would have thought it was Senator Obama coming to town. That was encouraging. For years I had thought Merlin was probably a Republican like our dad. Our family never talked much about politics around the family dinner table. But he and his wife had been supportive when I told them Candidate Obama was coming to our home.

I informed Dr. Zorba about the time, place, and requested donation. He suggested bringing his book *The Longevity Code* for a signing. What a great idea. It would be a gift for those attending the event.

Reality was setting in. A few days before the event, Jon told me that the Waupaca County Party hadn't held an event in some time. He wasn't sure how many people would be coming. After talking to Bonnie, Merlin was more optimistic. Bonnie had gotten good responses from her customers about Dr. Zorba.

On Valentine's Day, Zorba left Madison and drove his wife Penny, their full-size poodle, and me on the ninety-minute drive north to Waupaca. Along the way, Zorba discussed his speech. He said that he would use the term ACA—not Obamacare—in case there were some Independents who might be turned off by the more familiar term. He didn't want to politicize his talk. We talked about him signing the books included with the $35 donation. He liked the idea of taking questions after his talk. Over the years, Zorba had given many presentations nationally and internationally. He continues to meet with the Dalai Lama both in the States and India.

Forty-five minutes later, it started snowing. Then it started blowing hard. We were in a blizzard, with just a few cars and no trucks on the road. I was afraid that at any moment Zorba was going to want to turn back. I didn't realize at the time that he regularly drove to Colorado for family ski vacations. He was experienced at driving through snowstorms.

At one point on that drive during the blizzard, Zorba asked me what document did I think had the best soundbites? What kind of question was that during a blizzard?

I calmly said, "I have no idea."

He began reciting Abraham Lincoln's "Gettysburg Address" from memory. "Four score seven years ago, our fathers brought forth on this continent, a new nation..." "This was the first soundbite," he said. Zorba stopped at each phrase and let me think it through. It was quite profound and took my mind off the blizzard.

Hearing the beauty and wisdom of Lincoln's words made me emotional. I started to tear up. I was thinking, *Why is Zorba, this dedicated man, persisting to reach our destination?* By now, there were no other vehicles on the road with us. I was grateful he persevered. I would see this kind of fortitude again and again at all levels during the Obama campaign.

We arrived in Waupaca just a few minutes late. Even with the blizzard, thirty-five people filled the room. Zorba had dressed appropriately in his flannel shirt and wool lumberjack hat. People were excited to see him. He was engaging and demonstrated true empathy.

Zorba talked about the ACA. The audience was mostly older people, but the diner's staff was young, and they had also invited friends. Everyone was attentive and listened to his every word. Zorba did a masterful presentation on the importance of their health and the ACA. His book *The Longevity Code* includes a section on the importance of social interaction and community to one's health. He wove this central theme of the Obama campaign culture into his talk. There were numerous questions after.

Some of the audience members' questions criticized the government, and others commented that too much of their taxes were used for handouts. I could tell some of these folks were not Democrats. I was happy that Zorba had used the ACA term. We didn't want to alienate anyone. Obama needed Independent voters to win the state primary and the general election.

After the questions, and as part of their $35 donation, people produced their copy of Zorba's book *The Longevity Code* for him to sign. They appreciated that he stayed and took extra time. Checks were made out to "Obama for America." That was the only connection to the campaign, and no one mentioned or withheld their donation that night.

Because Bonnie had closed her diner that evening, Zorba signed a book for her too. She was so grateful. She quietly asked if he would autograph another book for a friend who couldn't attend the event. He did so graciously.

No one who'd gathered at Bon Marche seemed particularly concerned that we had driven through a blizzard. Apparently, they were used to that much snow. After all, it was February.

As Zorba drove back to Madison, we shared views of the event. All things considered, we agreed it was a success. "Should we do it again?" I asked. "Definitely," said Zorba. In my head, I began planning another fundraiser with Zorba.

At almost midnight, through the swirling snow, it was comforting to see the Madison lights.

The following day, I phoned a very happy Jon. He was a local hero, as the event had been Waupaca County Democratic Party's most successful event ever. We had brought in $1,400 for Obama. Jon said he had gotten nervous a few days before, discouraged by some of his calls. Some locals had said the event's price was too high.

When I reached Merlin, he said that a good number of people around town had heard about Dr. Zorba's visit and wished they had attended.

This successful fundraiser led to more statewide fundraisers. As Obama supporters, it gave us even more satisfaction and energy seeing what a difference we made for a handful of people. We wanted to do more, engaging more Wisconsinites.

Zorba did five more fundraisers before the general election in November. **O**

CHAPTER 6

Keeping the Faith in Pittsburgh

"We can complain because the rose bushes have thorns or rejoice because thorn bushes have roses."

—Abraham Lincoln

Zach Brandon's business off of State Street was the staging place for volunteers in a get-out-the-vote effort. Folks would sign in and pick up their VAN (Voters Access Network) lists, then go knocking on doors.

I had just returned with fellow volunteer Bruce after canvassing the near west side of Madison. Bruce worked for the state and was a dedicated and energized supporter of Obama's. We were just about ready to go back out again with a new VAN list when I met Renee. She and Bruce had just recently returned from a trip knocking on doors in Texas. They both had amazing stories and great energy. Renee and I hit it off right away and decided to keep in contact. About ten days later, Renee phoned and asked if I wanted to join Bruce and her for a road trip to Pittsburgh in the days before the Pennsylvania primaries.

I looked at my calendar. The next Obama fundraiser was planned for April 29 with friends. That would work. I would do all the planning with my friend Mary Ellyn Sensenbrenner and make the sponsor calls before I left.

I called Renee back, and she provided more details on the trip. Bruce was planning to fly in and out of Pittsburgh because of a time conflict. Also going along was Eric, captain of an Obama team named the Madison O's. Tom, a friend of Eric's, would be driving his Prius. Also coming was Joan, who had replied to an "Obama for America" email for Pittsburgh's primary volunteers. Renee instructed all of us to bring everything we needed for five or six days.

On a Thursday at six in the morning, Renee drove her mother's Westfalia van to my house. I was waiting with my new friend Joan, who lived just a few blocks from me. We headed to meet Eric and Tom in the Prius near the Beltline. Before we got going, we would stop in Stoughton to pick up two high school juniors.

A small town south of Madison, Stoughton was on the way. Eric had the address of one of the teenage boys' homes. When we arrived, both Blake and Neil were excited and ready to go. We all got out of the car to meet Neil's parents. They fully supported their trip.

Pennsylvania's Democratic primary was five days later, on April 22. With two stops for gas and bathroom breaks, we'd be on the road at least ten hours. It was 608 miles away.

The boys were going to write an article for their high school newspaper, *The Norse Star*, about their experiences in Pittsburgh working on the Obama campaign and canvassing. They would be missing four days of school, and I was surprised that was allowed. I surmised their teachers and parents must have been Democrats. I was also a bit surprised that their parents trusted us. Blake and Neil rode in Renee's van with Joan and me.

Even with GPS, we didn't arrive in downtown Pittsburgh until 9:30 that night. We were supposed to pick up keys to an apartment at a beauty salon, but it was already closed. We parked on the street in front, just in case someone was still inside. Tom called Billie, a backup contact person. Billie said he would meet us in fifteen minutes.

When we got out of the cars, we saw teenagers staring at us from across the street. After being in the vehicle for so long, getting back in was the last thing any of us wanted to do. We put on our Obama pins and placed Obama signs from a recent rally in our cars' windows. Renee had just happened to bring them along.

We heard police car's sirens wailing and lights flashing a few blocks away. A few of the kids walked by and looked at our signs. They saw we were wearing Obama pins. They appeared happy and surprised to see that we were Obama volunteers.

Billie arrived with a big smile on his face and couldn't have been nicer or more accommodating. When we asked Billie about the downtown neighborhood, he said we would be safe. Word had been put out on the street that Obama workers were not to be messed with.

We walked up the wide stairs to the second floor of the beauty salon building. The hallway was quiet and clean. It felt safe, even though an electrical cord was hanging from the ceiling with one light bulb.

Neil and Blake engaged Billie in a conversation about Pittsburgh's economic situation—a concern for many residents. Since the loss of steel jobs, the city had seen a steady exodus of people, and thus lower tax revenue. That forced the city to ratchet up taxes to keep city services constant, a trend that left many downtown buildings in disrepair. Property owners were short on cash and had many vacancies. Many residents also raised concerns over the integrity and trustworthiness of elected officials.

The next day all of us would face all those feelings when knocking on doors and talking to people.

Billie unlocked the door and let us in the sparsely furnished but large apartment. He was very excited and proud to be helping out Candidate Obama. He pointed out three bedrooms, a kitchen in the back area, and one bathroom off the living room. I took a peek at the tub, shower, and small sink. The bathroom was old but well taken care of. Billie gave us two sets of keys before departing to meet friends waiting for him. He said to call if we needed anything.

In the bedrooms were single mattresses on the floor with clean sheets. One of us was a camper, and the high schoolers had brought camping gear, including pillows, mats, a mess kit (plates, bowls, and utensils), and extra sheets and blankets. Renee, Joan, and I had not thought ahead and had been expecting beds and pillows. But everyone did bring towels.

All of us were exhausted and just wanted to sleep. We did what we needed to do and took turns using the bathroom. Right before we fell asleep, Bruce arrived from the airport. Within thirty minutes, we were comfortably zonked out. It was almost 11 p.m.

In the morning, we got up and dressed. One bathroom for three women and five guys sounds terrible, but it wasn't. Everyone was considerate and tidy.

From our collective experiences in Texas, Iowa, and Indiana, we knew there would be plenty of food at the volunteer office. We decided to check in at the Obama headquarters a few blocks away. We arrived to find a teeming office of organized chaos.

The main room area was loaded with staff and volunteers coming and going with canvassing sheets and brochures. We asked first for food and coffee and were directed to a room full of wonderfully smelling breakfast fare and the most welcoming aroma of freshly ground coffee. We had skipped dinner the night before and needed a good breakfast, so we loaded up our plates with eggs and grabbed cups of coffee.

It was Friday, and it would be a long day. After our meal, we grabbed power bars, junk food, cans of soda, and a few bottles of water for the day.

At the volunteer sign-in table, we were asked where we were staying. When we gave the volunteer the address, she was surprised. She asked us if we wanted different housing in a better neighborhood.

We figured that Billie didn't have the extra money to give to help Candidate Obama; providing a place for us to stay was a service he could provide. An effort had been made by him to make the apartment comfortable for us. We would be there for only four or five nights. We could get meals elsewhere, and for emergencies, there was a McDonalds and a Pick'n Save a block away. We wanted to stay at Billie's to respect his kindness.

We began knocking on doors with our volunteer packet of worksheets and brochures. On one of the handouts was a script of what to say at the door when someone appeared. There was a warning to never, under any circumstance, go into a house. This instruction was almost exactly what I had received in Indianapolis, but here it read, "Keep your partner with you at all times."

Eric, Blake, Bruce, and Neil went in Tom's Prius to a suburb called Plum. The high schoolers decided they would canvass with each other. The five other adults made up two teams. Joan and I went with Renee in her van to neighborhoods in the eastern and southern parts of Pittsburgh.

Our first day of canvassing proved to be a long day.

There were a surprising number of people home on a weekday. We were going door-to-door getting a feel for the registered Democrats in the area and their leanings toward which candidate: Clinton or Obama. The job was half informational and half persuasion. If voters were identified on our datasheets as undecided, they would be engaged in a conversation about what differences between the candidates mattered to them.

As you can imagine, not everyone was ecstatic to have random Wisconsinites interrupting their Friday morning with questions about politics. This is one of the largest challenges of this type of campaign work. Running into a supporter of the opponent isn't necessarily your biggest fear. It's the people who are completely turned off by politics in general who are difficult to engage.

Several of the neighborhoods we visited had not recuperated from the effects of NAFTA, the North American Foreign Trade Agreement that had opened up tax incentives for companies to move manufacturing to Mexico and overseas. Those neighborhoods were populated with union workers whose jobs had been shipped away. Residents found no reason to respect or participate in the political process. They had given up expecting help or change after years of past politicians who had made promises to them but with no results. That was the reason why out-of-town and state volunteers were asked to come to Pittsburgh.

Plum was a different story, with its large houses on good-sized lots. We found ourselves walking long distances to get to the front doors. Because Pennsylvania has closed primary elections, which allows only registered Democrats and Republicans to vote in their respective primaries, we were also trying to register new Democrats. There were few Democrats that needed to be registered and little chance to persuade anyone to vote for Obama in this wealthy area.

One woman in this well-to-do area told about her fear of talking politics with her neighbors. She asked us if she could see our data list to see which of her neighbors were Dems.

Even though the van had GPS, Joan, Renee, and I realized that we should have taken the map offered to us at the campaign office. Pittsburgh's streets were divided by three rivers—the Allegheny and the Monongahela, which then formed the Ohio River. On our assignment sheets, First Street house numbers could go from 100 to 1200, but some of those house numbers were on the other side of one of the rivers! This happened numerous times. We'd have to find a bridge, then re-find the street on the river's other side to finish our canvassing assignments. The campaign showed us the neighborhoods but not where the rivers were. It was confusing and exhausting to try to figure out how many of the sheets' addresses were on the same side of the river. A few times we stopped people on the street and asked for help with directions to the other side, but no one could ever really answer our questions. It could have been that they knew what we were doing and didn't want to help out the Obama campaign. (Renee had an Obama bumper sticker on the van.) But more than that, it seemed like the neighborhoods were incredibly insular. Not much was known about the streets on the other side of the river.

At the end of the day, Renee stopped in at the local supermarket close to our apartment to pick up snacks for us all. When she returned to the apartment with just two small bags, I asked why she didn't buy more.

"There isn't food in the grocery store." Renee had never seen anything like it. She had heard of urban food deserts but had no idea of the scope of the problem. She said the first things she saw were old fruits and vegetables. The boxes of food were all unknown brands, and the freezers were packed with gigantic bags of French fries and other foods than needed to be fried. There were aisles of frozen food, but the store lacked any nourishing or discounted food. Eric and Tom went out and got salads and pizzas for us.

After that first day, we were all bummed. In the living room of the apartment, we talked about our experiences. People didn't come to the door, and the ones that did seemed irritated. Some asked where we were from and didn't appreciate our northern accents.

Dogs were also an annoyance. Nearly every house in the East Pittsburgh area had at least one dog. One house on our data list had a brick porch closed in on three of the four sides. After we saw the all-too-familiar sign "Beware of the Dog," Blake walked up to the porch. He saw the dog was on a chain. But then he was surprised to find that the chain was longer than expected, and he was suddenly being chased off the porch by a little fluffy dog that bit him in the back of his calf.

We also had meaningful and rewarding conversations with a few voters who were on the fence. Eric had one absorbing conversation with a voter who was very much involved in local politics. She was serving on the borough's council, similar to a city council. She was well informed and asked thoughtful questions on relevant issues. He spent ten minutes with her, hoping she could go from there to persuading many of her constituents. Normally, most people had just one or two questions, and those conversations took only three or four minutes.

During our discussion, high school students Blake and Neil were quiet. When I asked Blake and Neil how their day went, I didn't get much of a reaction.

We collectively planned our tactics for the next day, wondering if we should talk to one of the volunteers or staffers at the campaign office before starting in the morning. Renee again asked Blake and Neil about their day.

The boys said that no one would talk to them. They got a lot of slammed doors in their faces. That was difficult to hear. Eric suggested that the boys join Renee, Joan, and me the following day.

On Saturday, April 19, we took two packs of canvassing maps from the volunteer office. Blake, Neil, Renee, Joan, and I headed to the south part of Pittsburgh. Renee would park the van in the middle of the street, and the four of us would take opposite sides of the street. On my first two knocks, no one answered.

The third one answered, and a woman looked out at us suspiciously. She listened and just took the information. I thanked her, but she didn't say anything and closed the door.

Blake knocked on the next door. After a woman answered, she took one look at him and slammed the door in his face.

"Holy smokes. Was this happening all day yesterday?"

"Yes," Blake said.

I thanked him for going out today and trying again. "It's not you," I told him. "Things are just different here."I took the next couple of doors and talked to a few people. Just one man seemed interested, but at least no one slammed their door. Blake wanted to try again. He wanted to do his part for the Obama campaign.

But once again, the door was slammed in his face! The same thing was happening across the street with Neil and Joan. After that, Joan and I did the knocking.

Later in the day, Renee dropped us off in an urban neighborhood. We had all been trying to think of better ways to engage people. I thought of the *Time* magazine that just arrived at our house the day before we left for Pittsburgh. I had planned to read it on the trip. Luckily, it was still in Renee's van. I grabbed it and brought it out on the streets with me. On its cover was a photo of Barack as a toddler with his mother—a typical mom and baby shot, both of them smiling and happy. I wanted to try something.

At our next address, the people were having a garage sale. Five women were standing around and chatting. I asked for the person whose name was on my roster.

She stepped forward. I think that she thought I wanted to buy something. I like garage sales, so my eyes were already scanning the items. I talked about the upcoming primary election. She listened for a few minutes, but after seeing the picture of Candidate Obama on my brochure, she noticeably began to tune out. I showed her the photo of Barack and his mom on the *Time* magazine cover.

She touched the magazine cover carefully and said, "Is this real? It isn't taped up, is it?" What an interesting remark.

I nodded. "It's real." I handed it to her.

She paged through it to make sure the magazine was authentic. She called two of her friends over and showed them the magazine cover. All three of them were excited to see it and looked at the magazine's article.

Another person crowded in to see the pictures inside the magazine. They began asking us questions, and I gave them each a campaign brochure. The woman whose name had been on my canvass sheet asked if she could have the magazine. I was thrilled. I replied that I'd give it to her only if, when finished, she agreed to pass it on. With a nice smile, she agreed.

Blake, Joan, and I left for the next house and phoned Renee. "When can you find a drugstore and buy more *Time* magazines?"She thought we were a bit crazy, but I told her what happened. We had made a breakthrough. With the *Time* cover, we had engaged not just one potential voter but five.

Renee arrived shortly after. She had gone to three different stores, always leaving two issues behind on the shelves so other customers would see it too. We hoped the magazine cover would help motivate potential voters to show up for the primary. We were energized. That afternoon went by quickly, and we had more successes. We continued to give out the magazine on the condition it would be passed along to friends and family.

After the rough morning Joan and Neil had, it got better that afternoon while using the magazine. Later in the day, Renee and Neil were invited into a house by a middle-class black man who wanted to show his wife the folks from Wisconsin. They were amazed that we would go around knocking on doors and talking to strangers. But when asked to volunteer for the Obama campaign, he said that would be strange and declined. It was disappointing and difficult to understand.

After finishing a long day, on the drive back to the campaign office, we talked about Neil and Blake being discriminated against because of who they were—most likely because of their age. It seemed important to discuss.

Renee, Joan, and I are all mothers, and we all had some comforting words to share. We told them how much we respected them for going out a second day.

I added, "Now you know how it feels to be discriminated against just because of how you look. You can better understand how other people feel when they get discriminated against or are a victim of being prejudged. Except, your experience lasted a few hours; for many others, it lasts a lifetime." It was a risky thing to say. Before working on this campaign, I would have never thought about framing the experience in such a way, but working on the Obama campaign had opened my eyes and heart. I wanted to share some of that experience.

The van started to make a dreadful sound.

Renee drove us to a service garage to get it looked at. When we pulled in, I noticed that two Latino mechanics had noticed the van's Obama bumper sticker, and they immediately got to work diagnosing and then fixing the problem.

A few minutes later, the owner came out of his office, and he too saw the Obama bumper sticker. Talking to Renee, he insinuated that the van wouldn't get fixed in his station.

But she would not be stopped. Renee turned on her charm and sweet-talked him, not letting him get a word in edgewise. By the time Renee finished talking and came up for air, the work on the van was almost done.

I remember the mechanics' smirks as they listened to Renee. They were working quickly to get the van fixed before their boss could change his mind. They were doing their part for Obama. Renee paid with cash, which had been part of her persuasive conversation.

After we drove off, the rest of us teased her about her Academy Award-winning performance.

At our evening wrap-up in the living room, we shared our experiences and our success with the *Time* magazine cover. Bruce and Eric had a rough day. They were in a lower-middle-class neighborhood where people felt that the upcoming elections had nothing to do with them. It seemed a waste of their time that Eric and Bruce were interrupting their day.

Eric and Bruce had felt like trespassers. Bruce felt these voters should have been approached months earlier by candidate volunteers or, better still, the candidate to show them that they did care about their plight. Emotions were running close to the surface after discussing the day's events.

Bruce had knocked on the door of a young woman who had heard of Obama. After discussing the issues and Obama's stand on several issues, she said she would vote for him. She was also interested enough that Bruce had offered to drop off Obama's book *Dreams from My Father*.

Bruce had brought along on the trip several of the paperback books for times like these. When he returned with the book thirty minutes later, her husband answered the door. Apparently, he had not been home earlier.

"I tried to explain but left in a hurry before I was physically chased out of their yard."

Eric had brought with him a copy of the "A More Perfect Union" speech that Obama gave after the Jeremiah Wright hoopla. That helped calm down some people who had been worried about electing an African American president.

When Bruce and Eric returned their canvassing papers at the end of the day, a campaign volunteer asked Bruce and Eric and our Madison team to attend a church service the following morning to give a talk about Obama. It was going to be at the Rodman Street Missionary Baptist Church, just a few blocks from our apartment.

We could sleep in since church didn't start until 10:30.

On Sunday,

we walked together to the morning service. It was a small, well-kept church surrounded by deserted cottage-size homes. The reverend was welcoming and gracious. The parishioners were dressed to the nines, with many women in hats. It reminded me of how my mother always wore a hat to Sunday church services.

I wanted to be respectful, but I was self-conscious that I didn't have something nicer to wear. They had a small but beautiful-sounding choir. Joan and the rest of us wished the service was longer so we could enjoy more of the choir's music.

Near the service's end, Bruce went to the front and spoke about the upcoming primary election on Tuesday. The campaign trusted him, and he had been instructed not to read a word-for-word statement. It was impressive to see how he spoke from his heart while still using the campaign talking points as guidelines. He engaged the parishioners as well as us.

In the afternoon, our band of Wisconsin volunteers had the good fortune of meeting Harold, a mailman originally from Mississippi. He was running a local canvassing operation out of his house and was thrilled that civil rights workers were at his home. He told his story about nearly being lynched in Mississippi. He was literally chased across the state line. Harold had come north to Pittsburgh and worked his way up to mail carrier. He was proud of his achievement but knew he was still being held back. He said there were many obstacles yet to overcome.

Seeing us show up to volunteer gave him hope. Harold joked, "Even white folks from Wisconsin are helping out." Harold made us feel like rock stars—a needed boost in the face of the general apathy we were encountering while knocking on doors.

We returned to knocking on doors and leaving voting information at the doors who didn't answer. We did engage with some folks who had planned to vote, and they appreciated the voting information.

With each day, we felt we were accomplishing more. Maybe it was a result of our straightforward conversations with the voters and our desire to make a difference. We were figuring things out and gaining confidence.

On Monday, the day before the vote, we were trying to cover as much ground as possible. We kept the sliding side doors of Renee's van open so Joan, Neil, Blake, and I could jump in and out like parachute jumpers as we cruised the streets, handing out information, leaving door hangers for all the doors with people who didn't answer.

That morning we landed in a trailer park. Blake and I took the lower half of the map; Joan and Neil took the upper part. Renee stayed with Joan and Neil. Their list was larger and more spread out.

Not too many people at the trailer park were home. The ones who did answer the door were surprised to see us, and a few were even talkative. At last, Blake was having some success.

Then we turned a corner and saw our next knock. This trailer had an old Confederate flag hanging outside of it. I sighed. The campaign said not to take risks, that our safety was always first. But it was midmorning, Blake had his cell phone, and Renee was no more than a few minutes away. All the names on our sheets had at one time voted Democratic.

I told Blake I would be careful. He stood on the side of me next to the wall of the trailer with his cell phone in his hand. The person answering the door would only see me.

After I knocked, I could hear a TV and a male smoker's gruff voice ask someone to go to the door. Slowly and carefully, a small girl opened the inner door.

I said, "Hello." She was about five years old and pretty, but she looked like she hadn't had a bath for quite a while. She turned from me and said, "Grandpa, there's a lady here."

"What does she want?"

The girl had beautiful, sparkling bright eyes. She asked me what I wanted, opening the door wider. I showed her the brochure and told her I was here to talk about voting tomorrow.

She repeated it all to the man. Now I saw he was an older man in a recliner, sitting with his legs propped up while watching TV. He turned down the sound. Another younger little girl was sitting near him, staring at me. She wasn't scared, just curious and shy.

I gave the girl at the door the brochure to give to her grandpa.

After taking it and giving it a look, he said, "I have seen this n— on TV." There was no anger in his voice. To him, the N-word was just another word.

I inhaled and said, "Yes, Obama has gotten a lot of publicity." I told him that the Pennsylvania primary election was the next day. I reminded myself I was in a different culture.

He asked me to come in. I said that I didn't have much time. He asked me why I was knocking on his door.

"I thought long and hard about going out and volunteering for Obama," I told him. "I was convinced our country would be better off because I felt I could trust him."

He kind of smiled and said, "Wouldn't that be something for a n—?" He went on to say that his daughter was at work, and he would give our pamphlet to her.

I thanked him and looked at this little girl, gave her a warm smile, and thanked her. As she closed the door, she finally smiled back at me.

She reminded me of why we were knocking on doors and why Obama was running for president. I knew that Obama would understand this situation, and they were part of why he was in this race. He had lived with children in poverty when he was young and in Jakarta with his mom.

I turned to Blake, who was a bit shaken. All I could say was, "I think he likes Obama, and he will give the brochure to his daughter." It was probably she who had voted Democratic and the reason this address was on our sheet. I took a deep breath and had to sort some things in my head.

In the afternoon, we canvassed in a more typical Madison-kind neighborhood of ranch houses with retired seniors and some families just a few miles from the trailer park. In the same routine, Renee would drive the van, and we jumped in and out. Joan and I were having some good conversations—

one with a family gathered on their front porch and another with a man taking a break from mowing his lawn.

He had seen us jumping out of the van and wondered what we were doing. He wasn't on our list. When we gave him a brochure, he grinned and was polite and put it in his pocket. Renee called for us; we had to leave. Joan and I wondered if he would consider voting for Obama.

We headed for the Petersen Events Center at the University of Pittsburgh, a basketball arena that seats over 12,500 spectators. When we had picked up our canvassing information from HQ, they asked us to return mid-afternoon. They needed volunteers to work a rally with Senator Obama that night.

A campaign worker said he expected they'd fill the entire arena, including the standing-room-only areas on the court. We were thrilled to be able to see Obama again. U.S. Senator Casey and U.S. Senator John Kerry, along with his wife, Teresa Heinz, would also be on stage. Senator Casey joked and said that he wasn't going to talk much. The audience laughed and he introduced Senator Obama. The crowd chanted, "Yes, we can!" Senator Obama teased about the Pittsburgh Steelers football team. Then he talked about being in Philadelphia where there was so much history about our country and core of our American ideals. Obama continued about how the Founding Fathers didn't want to settle for how things were, and they wanted independence from England. They wanted to have liberty and equal opportunities. They got together and worked to make these things happened. Our country has worked for, cried for, and bled for these ideals. We fought wars, including the Civil War, to keep these ideals alive.

Our job was to usher people to their designated areas. The campaign office volunteer was right; the arena was packed. The rally was exhilarating. It felt like a wonderful reward for knocking on the doors. The event went fast, though it lasted over an hour. It was energizing and the timing was perfect. Election Day was less than twelve hours away.

We brought food home from the rally and hashed over that day's activities. Blake shared the story of the man in the trailer park in the recliner and how we maybe persuaded him to consider voting for Obama. A man who hung a Confederate flag on his trailer had listened to us. We had shown him respect, and he had returned it.

It was April 22, Election Day.

We packed our clothes and belongings and loaded them in the car and van. We left the keys in the spot Billie had instructed. They would be there if we changed our minds and decided to stay another night.

At the district headquarters campaign office, the group received canvass information, along with more doorknob hangers with local voting info. The campaign volunteers asked us to return by mid-afternoon to drive voters who needed rides to the polls. There was concern about voter protection.

By this time, we felt relatively comfortable finding our way around Pittsburgh. All of the voters Renee drove to the polls were grateful for the rides. The voters were of all ages. Some brought their infants and kids because they didn't have babysitters. Joan drove an older gentleman with a turban who was so grateful for the ride that he was tearing up.

At 7:30, Renee called Eric and told him, Joan, she and I all headed back to the campaign office to drop off our materials. A volunteer thanked us for coming from Wisconsin and told us that the polls were tight. Eric, Blake, Neil, Bruce, and Tom joined us at the campaign office a few minutes later. Renee asked where the nearest campaign watch party would be.

The address the volunteer at the campaign office gave Eric and Renee looked like it was near the university campus. I would drive the van, and Renee would navigate. Eric located the place on the second level of a building.

We planned this as a quick pitstop where we would give and get some hugs, maybe share stories. We walked up the stairs and found eight people at the bar. Surely, we were in the wrong place, but we weren't. Where was everyone? hThey looked surprised to see us.

We had a Coke and caught the TV monitor. Obama and Hillary were neck and neck. It was 8:30 p.m., and we were ready to leave. We made a hasty exit, but once on the road, our adrenaline kicked in as we discussed our experiences. We were so distracted by our conversation that we didn't notice the lack of gas in the Prius until we ran out. It was one o'clock in the morning. We had been on the road for four hours and were nearly halfway home. Luckily, we saw the lights of a gasoline truck station in the distance. Renee brought enough gas to get us to the station. We only lost about an hour.

On the van's radio, we heard that Hillary won the Pennsylvania primary popular vote that night with 54.59 percent to a 45.41 percent. But she had not earned quite enough to catch up with Barack's national Electoral College's superdelegate vote. That kept him in the race.

We all remained determined to get to Madison and sleep in our own beds. Renee and Tom drove straight through the night.

Tom dropped off Blake and Neil in Stoughton. At sunrise, we arrived on the Madison Beltline and could see our beautiful Capitol building across Lake Monona and were thankful to be home.

None of us had regrets. We learned more about the challenges in getting out the vote, as well as discovering our strengths when creating solutions during canvassing. We had wonderful moments and surprises, too, like the Sunday morning service with the beautiful choir.

Eleven years later, the group fondly remembers our trip, reconnecting to help write this chapter. I want to thank everyone for searching through their memorabilia boxes and computer files. Thank you all for spending time on the phone with me helping to recreate this extraordinary experience for the Obama campaign. **o**

CHAPTER 7

Indianapolis Changed my Heart and Mind Forever

"Hope is the bedrock of this nation;
the belief that our destiny will not
be written for us but, by us."

—Barack Obama

My first National Finance Committee (NFC) meeting was scheduled for May 1, 2008, in a downtown Indianapolis hotel. That evening there would also be a meet and greet at the Indianapolis Museum of Art. Since I was new to the committee, Michael O'Neil had suggested that I attend the reception. The next day an orientation for new members would begin at 7:30 a.m. The regular meeting would start in the same room at 8 a.m.

After Michael had called with the details, I immediately booked my hotel room. It would be exhilarating to meet other fundraisers from the Midwest while also getting perspectives from other parts of the country.

In April, I had met an NFC member during a meeting at the national campaign headquarters in Chicago. Katherine Gehl had previously worked with State Senator Barack Obama on several assignments and was now a special project manager in the Chicago mayor's office. She and her father were 100 percent in support of Barack Obama. Her family had a lake home in southern Wisconsin, not far from Madison. She later contacted me and said she was coming to Madison before heading to the Indianapolis meeting. I offered her a ride.

Our five-hour drive went fast. Katherine shared wonderful stories about her experiences working with Senator Obama and meeting Michelle. She had also been to a couple of previous NFC meetings in Chicago. Katherine filled me in on what I could expect. It sounded exciting. Now I understood why Michael O'Neil was surprised that I didn't cancel my ski vacation in March.

That evening's reception at the Indianapolis Museum of Art was in its main room—too large for the number of people attending. Since I had been doing fundraisers, I had learned from experience that the size of the room was important for both the candidate and the attendees.

If a room felt empty, it was intimidating for the candidate. It looked like not all the invitees had shown up—their support substandard. Candidates running for national offices, like Barack, learned to respect the people who did show up for an event and not worry about why others didn't.

Attendees can easily feel the same way. Why does the room feel empty? Where are the other supporters? On such occasions, attendees may doubt or second-guess their support for the candidate.

Not this group. In spite of the flood of media coverage about Reverend Wright's fiery sermon, everyone was energized. The media had a frenzy over Obama's pastor, a clergyman who the media characterized as frustrated and cynical. Old videos were spliced and re-edited to make Pastor Wright look angry at America. The reverend seemingly professed just the opposite of what Candidate Obama was talking about in his campaign speeches. The Reverend Wright nonstop media barrage had happened not once, but twice. That was the second time around. Reverend Wright was the pastor of the Trinity United Church of Christ in south Chicago. For over thirty-six years, he welcomed and included the poor and the younger generation. His church congregation had grown from 250 to 8,000. The Obamas had been married in that church and their girls baptized. The reverend came into the crossfire of a political effort to bring down Candidate Obama. Sadly, the reverend retired later that year.

Entering the room at the Indianapolis Museum of Art, I recognized right away that, while friendly, this was a sophisticated group. Everyone was fully engaged and talking to someone else. I picked a small group of people closest to me who appeared enthusiastic about what they were saying.

Many of the men wore Italian suits. The women had on stunning cocktail dresses and expensive but not showy jewelry. When Katherine, my driving companion, entered the room, she looked radiant in a silk handprinted flowing dress. In spite of being underdressed, I felt welcomed and comfortable. Everyone gathered there was excited about the candidate. It was generally felt that Hillary would soon concede to Senator Obama.

In the conversations, everyone called the candidate "Barack," not using his title. These were Democrats who knew a lot about past presidential candidates and campaigns. I listened intently and found their insider stories insightful and entertaining.

Many of the guests knew each other from other Democratic campaigns. It was fun hearing stories of how they had met Barack. Many were from Illinois or had a connection to his first State Senate race. While some saw him lose to the incumbent U.S. Congressman Bobby Rush in 2000 in the Democratic primary, they kept the faith, believing in him. That was the only race that Barack Obama ever lost. Now everyone was convinced he could win the presidency.

When asked who I was and why I was there, I told them that Barack had been at my home in October 2007 for a fundraiser, and I had done six fundraisers before the Wisconsin primary, with more planned throughout the state.

They all knew that Barack won by 14 percentage points in the Wisconsin primary and congratulated me, which was a surprise. Of course, hundreds of others working in the field helped make that win. They were delighted that my events had been statewide, reinforcing the importance of fundraising and participation through the entire state. A few years later, Katherine Cramer wrote a book titled *The Politics of Resentment: Rural Consciousness in Wisconsin and the Rise of Scott Walker*.

Kathy spent seven years researching and talking to people in the northern part of the state. She is a professor in the Political Science Department at the University of Wisconsin. The book was widely read among Democratic and populist parties—both in the States and Europe, as well as by businesses like Google.

Besides bringing in money, fundraisers created memories cherished for a long time. Most high-dollar events were in private homes, where the media wasn't allowed. The atmosphere was comfortable, and the candidate could be sincere and plainspoken with their remarks and answers to questions.

Some wanted to know who I had supported in past presidential races. I had to be honest and said this was my first presidential race. My answer caught some of them off guard, and they were speechless for a few seconds. I almost blurted out, "I wasn't planning to be a Democrat," but that would be a distraction and maybe disrespectful to them.

They replied that they were happy to see a new face. Many also said attracting new people into the campaign was one of Barack's gifts. That was why the number of his supporters continued to grow.

One of the people I was talking with looked familiar. When I asked if he was Ned Lamont, the Democrat who had given Senator Joe Lieberman such a hard time, he smiled.

In 2006, Lamont beat the incumbent Senator Lieberman in the Democratic primary. This shock sent a message to incumbents in both parties: Don't get too comfortable and underestimate young, relatively unknown people who decide to run for national office. Lieberman went on to run as an

Independent and won. Ned Lamont became the governor of Connecticut.

The orientation was early the next morning at 7:30 a.m. With no stage or platform for the speaker, the hotel conference room was relatively small. The speaker—whoever it would be—would be standing just a few feet in front of us. There were eight of us new members in the front row. We were women of a wide range of ages. I thought there would have been more people there that morning.

The meeting started with Penny Pritzker, chair of the National Finance Committee. Penny had been in the news quite a bit. I was impressed that she was leading this small orientation session. After a short welcome, she had each of us give a brief bio of ourselves and tell why we had joined the campaign. She talked about the Obama culture, which was based on his community organizing experiences rather than traditional political strategies.

Penny said that we were helping our country during tough times. Most everyone around the world understood why we had gone into Afghanistan, but our image changed with the rest of the world and with many Americans when we entered Iraq and created a war. The economy was wearing thin, and our value structure seemed tilted. Change was needed.

Penny continued talking about the importance of Barack's expected wins in future states. The campaign was once again dealing with Reverend Wright's inflammatory sermon. Penny's remarks were honest, not sugar-coated. She was intense and no-nonsense—not harsh, just earnest.

Barack entered the small room and spoke to each of us. There was no rush. He must have done his homework because he personalized each conversation.

**I was surprised when he remembered our house and its packed rooms. He asked how my husband "Doc" was, and he thanked me for staying with him back in October when things had been rough. I was grateful for the kind words. I certainly had not expected to have a one-on-one with him. With the "respect, empower, include" creed, I felt I was back in the nonprofit world, where people were appreciated and trusted. He left the room and would return later.

The rest of the group joined us at eight o'clock. Penny summarized the briefings from the orientation. She added that David Plouffe, the campaign manager and expert pollster, was closely monitoring the poll numbers following the scrutiny of Reverend Wright's sermons. He would report to us shortly.

Suddenly Barack was crossing the room carrying a homemade (not perfect) chocolate birthday cake with one candle. One of the staffers ran after him with a cigarette lighter in hand. Once the candle was lit, everyone joined in with Barack in singing "Happy Birthday" to Penny.

She kept talking for a few more seconds. In disbelief, she saw what was happening. She was shocked that during this crucial, frustrating time of the campaign, Barack, his staff, or both had remembered her birthday and made the time to get a cake. Barack gave her a big hug and said something that made her smile. She departed the room with her cake.

Barack welcomed everyone. For a national campaign committee meeting, it felt like a small gathering. There were about a hundred people in the room. I wondered if the return of the reverend's controversy had kept some members home. The candidate spoke of how things were looking better. It was difficult to predict things when the media was so focused on one issue. He was saddened about the media starting up with the reverend. He conveyed that it wasn't fair to Reverend Wright. We all knew that politics was seldom fair. He called up David Plouffe for an update.

When David appeared, I was surprised to see how young and full of energy he was. David gave a brief analysis. This intense media focus on Reverend Wright's sermon could have broken the campaign's slow and steady uphill momentum, but David never stood still. He talked with passion and conviction. He said he would have more information in a few minutes.

Barack took questions from the group. Some remarked on other presidential campaign strategies and questioned why Barack's campaign wasn't using them. He defended his practices and nontraditional strategies to this seasoned political group of fundraisers. Some questions concerned the new idea of using social media. Was it working, and were those $5 donations on the website accumulating? As it turned out, social media changed the face of fundraising in the political world forever. It made the race more democratic, where everyone could participate and support their favorite candidate while also being very lucrative—with a $10 million day in September 2008 by Barack Obama. Also, the internet provided them with a priceless tool to appeal to newer and younger demographics.

David Plouffe bounded back into the room when Barack was answering. He stopped and gave the floor to David. With great joy, David announced that the polls—testing if Reverend Wright's story would strike a serious or fatal blow to Barack—had just moved up another four-tenths of a point, making a full point gain in our favor. He felt this was a firm move and would only increase when the poll numbers came in from Pacific states like California, Oregon, and Washington. There was great relief in the room. It was a difficult time, but this would be the last big hurdle regarding Reverend Wright's fabricated video.

The next day, David was proven right. I still get a chill writing about those few minutes. I was so glad to be in the room to witness these dynamics of public wisdom.

Penny re-entered the room while David was talking. Barack had a great smile and thanked us for our work and the work we would be doing. He was looking forward to seeing us again. Penny asked all of us to stay in Indianapolis for the rest of the day and join the inner-city Indianapolis field organizers. They needed help knocking on doors and making calls to voters. We needed to get out the vote of every Democrat or anyone who was on the fence and undecided if they would be voting for Hillary or Barack.

Local organizers were at a table outside the room. We were asked to sign up.

Almost everyone went to check in at the table. I was pleasantly surprised to see the men in the Italian suits taking off their jackets and silk ties and rolling up their shirtsleeves. They had energy and determination. It was all hands on deck—no matter how menial the task appeared to be. We would do anything and everything to get this exceptional candidate elected. We were there to help our country, not for any personal agenda or future job in the White House.

Seeing the devotion of the NFC members and quality and sincerity of Barack's staff at that meeting was a turning point for me. When I heard that there was a need for more volunteers for canvassing, I reserved another night at the hotel.

The primary was just a few days away on May 6. Because I had a car, I received my assignment and driving instructions for canvassing an area on the north side of the city.

I drove to a well-maintained, lower-middle-class apartment complex. When I parked my car, I got out and headed to a freestanding building that looked like a community center. A homemade sign near the front entrance read: "Welcome Obama Volunteers." Once inside, I found that I was the only white person in the room. A smiling black woman behind the table looked a bit surprised at my entrance. I told her that I had been at a National Finance Committee meeting downtown for Senator Barack Obama. I was assigned to this location for GOTV. She summoned another woman.

Miss Gloria was in charge. She asked me to come to her table in the middle of the room for the canvassing information. I told how her how I was assigned to this neighborhood. I added that I had a fundraiser for Candidate Obama in my home. I had also knocked on doors in the Iowa primary. She was a bit surprised but was gracious. Miss Gloria explained who lived in the complex. She told me that there was a wide range of ages among residents. Many people had lived there for a long time, and voting was important to the residents.

I didn't know the Indiana state voting laws. I thought of my trips to visit my daughter at the University at Bloomington. When I was driving there, I saw Confederate flag bumper stickers on pickup trucks.

She continued with information about knocking on doors, explaining the voting site was this community center. She mentioned issues people might ask about and gave me a list of the identifications local voters needed to show before they could vote. She gave me a colorful printed handout with a picture of Senator Obama on it.

Looking me square in the eyes, Miss Gloria said, "Mary, if people don't come to the door or if they are short with you or maybe discourteous, it's because when white folks come to our doors, it's always with bad news. It most likely is a truant officer, social caseworker, police officer, or a detective."

Her words went to my core. They made sense. I thanked her for being candid. It was important information for me to understand so I would not get discouraged or take it personally.

She said to be sure they see the brochure cover with Obama's picture on it. She asked if I knew about REI.

"I sure do, from knocking on doors in the Iowa primary. Also, I'm a community organizer."

She smiled and offered food and drink. I appreciated her hospitality and had lunch.

Because of the apartment complex's design, I could walk to the apartments. Like in Iowa, my paperwork had a listing of the names, addresses, ages, and genders of those to be contacted. I had just over forty doors to knock on. Based on the last presidential elections, these were the residences of probable

Democratic voters. There was a small scale of options. As in Iowa, I was to make an "x" for NH (not home), NA (no access), or M (moved). The last question was which candidate the person would vote for.

The first door is always the hardest no matter where you are. I knocked and no one answered. I left a brochure.

Then, a second knock. No reply.

At the third, a TV was on. The door opened, revealing an unfriendly face. Before I could say anything, the woman demanded to know what I was doing at her front door.

I held up the Obama brochure. She looked at me, then at the brochure, and appeared puzzled.

I asked if she would be voting, but she wouldn't answer. I told her I was volunteering for Obama, that he had been at my house.

She was having a hard time, maybe because it sounded so unbelievable. Why would a white woman who had the famous black candidate at her house be at her front door? When a man joined her at the door, he too looked angry. I said I would leave the brochure and pointed to the printed voting place and the date.

I decided not to use the line that the candidate was at my home. If the shoe were on the other foot, I probably wouldn't believe that myself either.

At the next door, I knew they were home because the TV was on. After knocking, I could see people moving through the door's small window. I left a brochure and a handwritten message: "Sorry I missed you. Hope you will vote. Mary." I really wanted to connect.

What Miss Gloria had said to me at the community center was ringing in my head, and I was again thankful for her guidance. A few people did answer their doors when I knocked. Their eyes would tear up, saying, "Why would someone like you [a white person] volunteer for Obama?" I told them I had read his book *Dreams from My Father* and had met him. I continued that his message—of not being a red state or blue state but a united country—was important for our future. He spoke from his heart, and it felt authentic to me. I wanted to do my part and help make him be our president. I trusted him.

I also shared that Obama had left a lucrative law practice and gone to work at the South Chicago Community Center as a community organizer. I know his values were in the right place, that he would never "sell out" for personal gain. Money was not a motivator for him. He reminded me of a phrase my father would reassuringly say at times: "If you do the right thing, things will work out." I felt in my gut that Obama was running for the right reason: to make our country better for us all.

A few heard my accent and wanted to know where I was from. I am not sure which words triggered their comment. They just knew that I didn't sound like someone from Indiana. When I said Wisconsin, they asked who paid for my gas for the car or who was paying me to knock on doors. They could hardly believe that I was doing this on my own. No one was paying me any money or offering me any favors. Many times, I ended by saying, "There are a lot of people like me who are volunteering for him throughout the country." I wanted to give them hope. I was glad to be doing this work. It felt fulfilling, like I was making a difference for the people with whom I talked. We had some open and straightforward conversations, which was rewarding. It felt like hope was real. As a friend in Madison told me, "Mary, you had an awakening." I could only hope the people on whose doors I had knocked did too.

One person I met that day will stay with me forever. Before she opened the door, I heard her rubber-soled slippers scraping a plastic floor runner on the other side of the door. The door barely opened. I saw one yellow eye, just a part of a face of leather and gray hair. I held up the Obama brochure, and she opened the door two more inches. Short and bent over, the woman had deep wrinkles from the sun on her face. Her fingers were thick from years of hard labor.

Her hands reminded me of old farmers' hands in my hometown, but these hands were more gnarled. She was shaking her head no.

I spoke a little louder. Maybe she didn't hear me the first time. "There are many thousands of other people like me who are working for Barack Obama. We want him to be president. We are working hard for him."

Her head stopped shaking no. She looked me straight in the eye. With the saddest eyes I had ever seen, she said clearly, "If he gets to Washington, they will tear him apart, limb by limb. I don't want that to happen to him."

A shiver came over me. I pictured what she might have seen, maybe as a child or an adult. I had heard stories from blacks about why they had moved their families north. It was domestic terrorism that we white folks could not even imagine. No way could we understand this part of our country's history. It will be a painful journey for this country to truly come to terms with its bloody history of racism and demonizing a people. This will be a journey well worth taking so that we can move on and keep our country united.

I tried to reassure her that too many cared about Barack Obama. If he won, he would have a majority of the country behind him, and things would be okay. Looking down at the colorful brochure, she took it from my hand and nodded goodbye.

I walked slowly to the next door, trying to take in her words. She couldn't be right, but she was so certain. I didn't know her past. She could be the granddaughter of a slave or a sharecropper. I didn't know what this woman had witnessed or endured.

After four hours of knocking on doors and talking to people, I experienced a humility that I had never felt before, as well as an entitlement that I'd taken for granted.

When I returned to the community center, the gracious volunteer Miss Gloria was still there. She took my paperwork to tally its results. She offered me food. All of a sudden, I was ravenous. I joined a table of black women who had also been knocking on doors.

We shared stories of canvassing. We all were working for the same candidate, the same cause. We had a frank conversation about the possibility of Barack Obama winning. Was our country ready for a black president? Or was Obama too white with his Harvard/East Coast education, growing up in Hawaii where the Asian and Samoan population had mixed fairly easily? That state didn't have any of the indoctrination of post-Jim Crow and the Reconstruction era. Did he have enough political experience, or was he too young? Still, all of us at the table remained optimistic and hoped he could win. That was why we had volunteered. It felt like I was with kindred spirits.

One of the ladies, Miss Thelma, was especially curious about what kind of reaction I had received when door knocking in the neighborhood. I told them of the disbelief from most of the people who opened their doors and saw me. I relayed their remarks on being a volunteer, and how I told them that no one had paid me for gasoline or for my time. I decided to tell them that Candidate Obama was at my home. They wanted to hear more about the fundraiser, and it was wonderful sharing that extraordinary time with them.

They were all working or retired women and mothers. Some with grandchildren said that they were working for their grandchildren's futures. Having a president who looked like them would instill hope in the next generation of black children. For the last couple of months, they had attended rallies, raised money, recruited volunteers, and worked with young people for Senator Obama.

I decided not to tell them about the older gray-haired woman with the slippers at one of the doors, who could not vote for Obama. It would be too sad, and I didn't want to jeopardize their energy and optimism. The Indiana primary election was just four days away.

One woman, Miss Betty, spoke about committee meetings with both blacks and whites at the table. She said that when she would be at a school meeting or a parent conference meeting and she would complain about something hurting black kids or her child, or if she focused on a perceived black issue, the white people's eyes would glaze over. It was as if they were saying, "Here it comes again, more complaining. Why can't you people just be satisfied? Are things really that bad?"

I shared that I served on a fair amount of city and community meetings and witnessed the same phenomenon.

Miss Betty said the messenger made a difference. In a group or during a committee meeting, if a white person brought up something about a black issue or concern, the other whites in attendance accepted it much more readily. They would ask questions and engage in a discussion on the topic. A solution was more likely to happen.

A few months later, I tried out the idea that the messenger makes a difference.

The next day I returned to the same complex and knocked on more doors. Because of my Wisconsin accent, I was deemed ineffective on phone calls encouraging people in the area to get out to vote. I had learned yesterday about the experience of a white person at the doors of this complex and the time it took to build a rapport. A black voice would be trusted and was needed to make the calls efficient. That was okay with me. We wanted to make our efforts effective. Every vote was important.

I felt I had made a connection the day before and wanted to talk with more people. I arrived early. The same gracious woman, Miss Gloria, was at the community center. We ate breakfast together while awaiting the delivery of the canvassing paperwork. I spoke to her about the older woman who had made such an impression on me.

She was saddened but unsurprised. She said the older generation had been through a lot. They knew stories of their ancestors who were educated and elected to local and congressional offices before Jim Crow and the Reconstruction era. All that would come to a halt when the segregation laws of Jim Crow passed at the federal level. After the federal law was enacted, the black people mainly in the South lost nearly all their civil rights. Harsh realities and changes followed. Social activities in the southern urban states with the good jobs and opportunities were abruptly shut off because of the fear of white and black adults and children mingling.

She continued with her own stories of being excluded at work and other social activities, like shopping in a store and being followed by a security officer who assumed she would steal something. She would never try on clothes and put them back on the rack.

I had been in retail in an executive management program in the dress department in a well-known downtown Chicago department store and had spent a lot of time on the sales floor. I had never served black customers. They weren't there. At that time, I had met just a few American blacks and a few blacks from the Caribbean. All had been students at the University of Wisconsin.

Miss Gloria spoke of her work in an office and how a black person rarely gets a second chance. When a white person makes a mistake, there's always an excuse: they were having a bad day, the machine broke, the manager gave the wrong instructions. When the same thing or something similar happened to a black worker, comments like, "I told you so," were muttered with rolling eyes, or, "What do you expect from those people?"

That was painful to hear, but I knew she was speaking the truth.

She went on about her daughter who returned from school one day, frustrated with a teacher's comments about how to apply for a job. The teacher apparently had no clue that there were always more questions and more judgment for black interviewees. Asking questions about the company or the job position, as this teacher urged, could make a young black woman appear uppity, maybe aggressive. Black applicants had to know their place.

She told her daughter, "White people just don't understand. How could they?" But she also told her daughter, "Be kind and try to understand them."

Those words of wisdom and patience stayed with me. I share them in conversations when I think white people will be accepting and understand. Sometimes I miscalculate, and people feel uncomfortable. Still, I never regretted sharing Miss Gloria's kind and forgiving words.

The canvassing paperwork arrived with the potential voters and addresses. The door-knocking was more routine the second day. Also, I knew what to expect. It was easier engaging people in conversations. I could answer their questions better and felt more comfortable. After twenty-five or so doors, I had to return to Madison. There was yet another fundraiser in the works.

The five-hour drive back to Wisconsin was a good time to recall and reflect on the intensity of the past three days—from the fancy museum reception to the meaningful talk with the gracious volunteer at the community center. Would I ever see

Miss Gloria again? She was a wise woman. I wanted to let her know that her advice would stay with me forever.

I also learned another lesson. We never know how we affect and nurture the people around us. There is a reassuring feeling that we are remembered for the good things we share with others that can enrich their lives. It could be a memory that they recall that helps them find a new path in their life, or maybe just a reprieve from a difficult situation.

On May 6, we lost to Hillary in Indiana, but only by 1.12 percent of the vote. Hillary had 50.56 percent and Barack 49.44 percent. That same day, Candidate Obama won North Carolina with 56 percent of the primary vote. After those two primaries, superdelegates started to engage and vote for Obama.

The next day, the coverage started to sound upbeat about Obama. It felt very good, but there were still four more weeks of canvassing and getting out the vote.

A year later, I took the chance on Miss Betty's experience and theory that the messenger made the difference. The test came at a thank-you dinner for sponsors of one of our congressional legislators. The event was in one of the University of Wisconsin's buildings. Along with the legislator, there were about twenty donors at our table. All were older professors, some researchers, and some businesspeople.

After the main course, one of the businessmen started to complain about "those people," referring to the black section of Madison. He said they were bringing down our kids' reading and math scores for the entire city. "We have poured so much money in that area, and still there is complaining. What can we do about it?"

It was a demeaning and snarky tone. I was hoping that a black person was there to give some pushback but then realized he would not have said those crass words if there was a black person present at the table.

Sitting across the table from me, the legislator in attendance made cautious remarks, saying this was Madison, one of the more liberal and progressive cities in the nation. We were doing plenty for minorities; it was just a matter of time.

My blood started churning. I remembered the conversation in Indianapolis about how the messenger makes the difference. Then I remembered a conversation when I was the campaign chair for a new community center.

While giving a tour of the building to a person new to town, I casually asked her how she liked Madison.

She was a beautiful African American executive from a Fortune 500 company. She had just married a white man who worked in the University's administration. While finalizing things at her job, she had made six appointments with a Madison realtor.

She met the Madison realtor in the University professor housing area. The realtor had appointments at two homes for sale. By the time she got out of the car and to the front door, oddly, the house was just put under contract. The other house down the street also happened to be sold suddenly. After two hours of looking at homes in other areas with similar results, the realtor drove her to the black section of Madison.

I shared this woman's story now with guests at the table. I also mentioned that in big cities, blacks have learned to sound white on the phone. It was a learned practicality to avoid being prejudged. It made a difference in their success.

The room got quiet and uncomfortable. I was happy that at least most of us were finished with dessert.

The legislator leaned into the table and eyeballed me, asking directly, "Mary, when did this happen?" They had a gotcha tone, thinking this situation was back in the 60s or 70s.

"Four years ago."

There was a gasp of shock in the room, and the legislator appeared dumbfounded.

"This is why those people are still complaining," I said cautiously but firmly. Talking to the businessman and the congressional legislator, who I liked, had been difficult. It was out of character for me, but my experience in Indianapolis with Miss Gloria and the other black women at the community center had given me the courage to speak up. They were right. Their stories had given me the confidence to share that story many times in many venues when we Madisonians thought we were so progressive and liberal. To their credit, many at the table that day saw it as a learning experience. O

CHAPTER 8

Fundraisers Are Not All About Money

"Fundraising is not about making a donation, it is about making a difference."

—Kathy Calvin,
CEO of the United Nations Foundation

Most people are nervous about throwing fundraisers, especially in private homes where, not incidentally, they are especially successful. With three or four good volunteers, an event in somebody's house can be much easier to pull off while also raising more money.

In 1991, my friend Lisa got a job in Senator Feingold's campaign office. Wanting to make a good impression, she called me: "Can we have a fundraiser at your home? Russ Feingold is running again for state senator." She promised to bring the food and would send out the invitations to my friends, along with others on the campaign list. It sounded fairly easy.

She wanted me to open up my house for a fundraiser for Wisconsin State Senator Russ Feingold, someone I did not know at the time. But I may have known his sister. I asked if the senator was related to Nancy Feingold. I knew Nancy as one of my customers at The Peacock, a store I owned. She stood out because of her ever-present and engaging smile. My friend put me on hold. In a minute, she hopped back on the phone.

"Yes, that's his sister."

"Well, if he is half as nice as Nancy, I will do it." I went to my calendar, and we found a date.

I cleaned the house the day before. My teenaged daughters, Niki and Muffy, helped out. A Feingold campaign staffer called and asked when they could bring over the food and drinks and the plates, napkins, and utensils. Did I have a large Coleman cooler for the drinks? Yes, we did, and I could get another from my next-door neighbor. She said that the response had been larger than expected, which was a good sign.

The next day, five staffers and my friend arrived with everything. I decided that the food would go on the dining room table with the plates, napkins, and utensils. The drinks would be on the back porch for a better flow in the house for the guests. The weather was hanging on—overcast, but no rain. Our open porch was still useable and comfortable. The kitchen was the holding place for extra food. Replenishing food would be easy; that became my job.

When my daughters, Niki and Muffy, arrived home from school, they were overwhelmed to see so many people setting up the event at our house. A registration table was set up, and guests started to arrive. The fundraiser started at five o'clock.

The girls hung out and helped for a while until guests were filling the house, then they retreated to their bedrooms.

The living and dining rooms were filling up, and some people went to the back porch for beverages. We had just completed some remodeling and added an open elevated back porch to have an outdoor dining area and a better view of Lake Mendota. Our backyard had a small lot—smaller than the house. The new porch was hospitable, and some guests migrated out to the porch and backyard.

A few days before, there had been a small article in the paper about Senator Feingold considering a run for the U.S. Senate, which resulted in some buzz among the guests. When Russ arrived, he looked happy and impressed with the house and the setup. He mingled and the guests were engaging with him. I could tell he had loyal supporters. About half an hour later, Russ decided to give his talk on the back porch. His staff ushered the guests outside into the backyard.

Russ thanked everyone for the fundraiser and updated the guests on issues like the bovine growth hormone—an important issue for Wisconsin's dairy farmers. He slowly switched gears, then announced that after much thought and talking to supporters and other politicians, he would be running for U.S. Senate. The guests were thrilled to be the first to know. Many wanted to help out, and others wrote another check.

The event was a resounding success, and we had even exceeded his campaign's financial goal by $1,000. Two days later, the exciting announcement of the senator running for national office in the U.S. Senate hit the media. For Hans, Niki and Muffy, and me, it was exciting to see Russ's announcement in the morning newspaper and be among the first to know.

After Russ's announcement, a number of people at the gathering asked me about future fundraisers. They wanted to support him and asked who they should contact. I gave them my name and called over Lisa to meet them so she could flag their names as sponsors for future fundraisers and events.

Years later, I would greatly appreciate Obama's campaign introducing software for political campaigns and outreach. That technological progress has empowered me to reach more supporters and voters.

As the Feingold campaign staff was breaking down the event and cleaning up the house, there were many thank yous followed by, "Can we come back next year?"

Without hesitation, my answer was yes. Hans and I were impressed with his education, as a Rhodes scholar, and his views on the issues and his wonderful connection with his supporters. I had anticipated their question and had already collected some of our guests' names and contact information.

In the years that followed, Hans and I sponsored two fundraisers a year: one for a community nonprofit that we felt was doing exceptional work, and the other for a politician whom we agreed with on their core values and stand on issues.

As time passed, I started to get more involved with organizing each of the events, specifically the food being served and the room setup. I used many of my mother's dinner party ideas and recipes. Later, the offerings evolved to finger food, saving time and money on forks and spoons. Also, it avoided the trials of women and their purses, balancing a glass of wine, a plate of food, plus utensils. Discarding the need for a fork or spoon might be a small matter, but little things like that can make an event more enjoyable and conversations go smoother.

My mother always followed a theme or used the current holiday to guide her table decorations. Both a chosen theme and the weather made a difference in how my mother planned her menus. These small touches personalized any gathering she hosted. People noticed such things, and I followed her example for our events. (See the epilogue for more information, ideas, and lessons learned from various fundraising events.) For our gatherings, I focused on an issue or idea related to the candidate. It could be as simple as making "M" cookies covered in Democratic blue frosting for U.S. Congressman Mark Pocan's annual Farmers Market Fundraiser.

Also, I tried to make my events give something back to the donors. Being in retail and having my own business for so long—nearly thirty years—I had a habit of giving people something in return when they handed over their money. Also, I grew up in a farming and factory community and had seen how hard people and entire families worked. This line of reasoning kept me from begging or just plain asking for donations. It never felt good just taking people's money. Giving donors something in return made sense to me, such as delicious and well-presented food, an opportunity to get to know an exceptional political candidate, networking, or maybe just a wonderful memory of a welcoming social gathering.

Nearly everyone wants to make a difference or wants to be part of something bigger than themselves. This core idea is the key to my long life of fundraising in Madison.

Also, when phoning and issuing invitations, I never took "no" personally. Whatever reason given for their reluctance or objection, I would accept without judgment. And if they said "no" with no clear reason, I would ask if I should keep calling them. In most cases, it was something in their personal lives that made them say no—not me or the candidate or the cause. It was simply bad timing. I didn't hear or figure out some of these rejections until months later. I realized how important it was not to jump to conclusions. Some of the reasons I would later find out about from friends or from them were personal, like going through a divorce, receiving a life-threatening diagnosis, loss of their job, etc.

Whenever I see those people at social activities or in the grocery store, I am always friendly with a smile, and we engage in small talk. It has been forty years of fundraising in Madison. Being a volunteer is also a reason for this longevity. I always picked the projects and candidates who I felt I could believe in. There is no burnout when you have passion for a cause or candidate and a likelihood of success that builds confidence.

After Candidate Obama was in Madison in 2007, and after he won the Iowa primary and continued winning other state primaries, calls came in from more Madison area candidates and nonprofits. There was some cachet about having their fundraiser at the same place as the popular presidential candidate.

After the success of that event, I decided to use the Obama format for future political fundraisers. He raised the standard. I had witnessed the excitement and sincere appreciation of volunteers who had their picture taken with the candidate. Obama welcomed selfies after the program. Taking questions from donors made them feel engaged and respected. It was a real exchange with the candidate.

Obama had used only an index card to thank Hans and me and to do a shout-out to some of the sponsors who knew him from the Chicago law firm. He did not use a script for his fifteen-minute talk. He spoke from his heart and with honesty. If he could do that when he was twenty-three points below Hillary, I felt our state candidates owed it to their donors to have the same level of interaction. In many cases, the state candidates knew their donors. Events with them were more like family gatherings. That was Obama's respect-empower-include strategy in practice.

Early on, when organizing future fundraisers with this new standard, I was surprised to get pushback from some Wisconsin campaign staffers, with responses like "If we have time, we'll do the photos with the volunteers and take questions." They wanted their candidates to give their stump speech; it was one-way communication during the program.

I told them to make the time. Volunteers deserve to be thanked. They save campaigns considerable amounts of money by donating their time. And donors deserve to be acknowledged. I shared my experience with how the donors had responded so enthusiastically when being allowed to ask Obama questions. At events I organized, candidates needed to be available for at least three questions from the donors. Also, no scripts or prewritten speeches. People were tired of them. It feels disrespectful and strange that someone needs to be prompted while connecting with their home base, especially the candidates running for re-election. By then, they should know the issues and have the confidence to interact.

A few times after I got pushback from a campaign, I told the campaign finance director to think it through with the candidate and call back the next day or two with their answer. They and the candidate had thought it through, and in nearly all cases, this new approach made sense to them. We went on to set a date.

Twice I held fundraisers at which political candidates arrived, and their lead staffer stated right away that the candidate would need to leave early. I asked, "How early?" "Fifteen to twenty minutes."

"Okay," I answered. "We will start the program fifteen minutes early."

I took the candidate directly to the kitchen for photos with the volunteers, and I saw the dismay on this staffer's face. But soon after that, I started the program early. After thanking the volunteers and the sponsors and acknowledging the other elected officials in the room, I told our guests that we were starting a few minutes early so the candidate could stay on their schedule while still taking at least three of their questions, which the candidate did. The candidate did a great job—maybe even surprising themselves and their staff.

The question and answer part of the program has been the most exciting and memorable part of many of our fundraisers.

The donors are like family, most asking well-thought-out questions and others adding humor. Many times, a question prompted a candidate to add a forgotten detail, or they get a chance to bring up another important issue. It became a true exchange. Over the years, all the questions have been courteous and sincere—with one exception.

A few years ago, at an event, I noticed a man was not mixing with the others. During the end of the program and after several other questions, he asked a question in a snarky tone. I asked him to speak louder so we could hear his question. He said the question. It was a strange and non-consequential question that was intended to be a gotcha moment. The other guests reacted with silence and murmuring, but the candidate remained calm and did okay.

I interjected by saying we had one more question. The candidate picked one of the guests, and the program ended on a high note.

It was my home, and I felt that I had the right to ask this man who he was and how he came to be there. When I approached him, I noticed he was not wearing a name tag. When I asked his name, he said a friend of his had been unable to attend and had told him to take his place.

I asked who his friend was. Later I did find his friend's name on the paid donors list at the registration. It had come from the candidate's email list. Well, I don't know what got into me and why I was pursuing this interaction. Maybe it was because I had been a political candidate and had felt the sting of this kind of disrespectful approach. I told him that I hoped he would be more sincere in the future when he would be asking questions from another candidate. He barely looked at me and headed to the door.

The vetting of candidates and timing of fundraisers has proven very important over the years. Also, not overusing my Obama email donor list was essential.

People appreciated my short, personalized messages and carefully prepared invitations—always designed to be attractive. My invitations always had different formats and designs that reflected the candidate. Many times, I would work directly with the campaign's graphic designer, which was the most efficient, or with the finance director. The intent was to grab the attention of the person opening the email and have their curiosity sparked and read the information. Presenting an issue with a unique appeal or showing a candidate in a new light gets people interested, too. I remember our U.S. Congressman Mark Pocan at the Rock County party event after a tough election cycle. After hours of discussing and analyzing election losses, the people in the room were quite gloomy and worried.

Then Mark did a magic trick, and like magic, it lifted their spirits. After his trick, and accompanied by hopeful and positive commentary, the folks in the room were smiling. Some were laughing. Mark had provided them with joy, maybe hope. When Mark asked me to hold a fundraiser for him, I said that I would, on one condition; at the event, he had to perform his best magic trick.

And he has, for every subsequent annual fundraiser we've held. Through the years, Mark has become quite impressive with the caliber of his magic.

Candidate Obama in my living room for a fundraiser, October 15, 2007.

The magazine cover that opened conversations when knocking on doors in Pittsburgh.

Wisconsin volunteers in Pittsburgh, with Joe the mailman, who fed us and shared a hair raising story, about literally running out of the south to save his life.

In Denver in Mile High Field, nominee Barack Obama would be giving his acceptance speech as the Democratic Candidate for President.

Dr. Zorba Paster (with the mustache) volunteered his time to be the headliner for many fundraisers. Surrounded by Wisconsin donors and volunteers on January 20, 2008.

At a typical "round table" one hour is allowed for questioning for the President. After being in five of these kinds of gatherings, he never once needed prompting from staff.

I have had hard lessons to learn too. One was to stay out of Democratic primaries. If I chose a candidate during a primary and they lost, some of the other candidates harbored hard feelings towards me. Some think that I played a part in them not winning. Now before throwing fundraisers, I let the Democratic voters make the decision in the primary elections. I focus on the general election and winning against Republicans, not other Dems.

Unless you have deep pockets and an open calendar, there simply isn't time or resources to get involved in every county and state election. I made a big commitment to the national elections and had success with Senator Obama's campaign.

I decided to steer clear of local elections except for the Madison mayor's nonpartisan election. I ran for mayor in the mid-1990s, have served on many committees, and chaired a number of downtown projects. I remain devoted to the city's future. Luckily, the mayor's elections are on a different political cycle than national elections. The mayoral election is in April every four years.

Many years later, one fundraising strategy sprung from an extremely successful event with U.S. Congressman David Obey. That year there were four state senator candidates running for election that we wanted to support. John Lehman was up for re-election, and there were also three new candidates in three different districts: Kristen Dexter, Donna Seidel, and Lori Compas.

I had received calls from all the women who wanted me to do a fundraiser for them. I thought that all three had a good chance of winning. They were organized, smart, hard-working, and their motivation was to make life better for their districts. I decided to hold an event with all of them and hoped we could get U.S. Congressman Obey to be the headliner, drawing an even bigger crowd. The event had to do well since it would be divided four ways with the four candidates. He was the well-respected chairman of the House of Representatives Committee on Appropriations. That formidable committee regulated expenditures of money by the government. It is one of the most powerful of all the congressional committees, and its members are rightly seen as influential.

I called Obey's campaign office in Wausau, his home base. They liked the idea of having several candidates at a fundraiser. After they contacted the congressman, they sent me his cell number.

I was surprised. Maybe he was curious and thought I might instead hold a fundraiser for him. Frankly, I had thought he would say no to the group event. When we spoke, I was ready with one more persuasive reason why he should do the fundraiser.

But he said yes. We worked around his schedule and found a Friday and Saturday that would work for him. Now with frequent airline service, most of the congressmen and women return to their congressional districts on most weekends. It is better for their personal lives. At one time, congressmen and women would move to Washington, D.C., for their terms.

I told him that we would have a driver pick him up at the Milwaukee airport. After being driven to Madison, he could stay at my home for the night. We had a large private bedroom and bath upstairs. No kids, no pets. (Niki and Muffy had since moved away.) The congressman could rest or work.

He had written a book called *Raising Hell for Justice*. I asked him if he would sign copies of his book for the guests and volunteers.

Yes, he would.

When I made my sponsor calls, I asked them if they had his book. If so, and if they wanted it signed by the congressman, could they drop it off at the house by Friday, the day before the event? Their suggested inscription should be inside on a post-it with their name.

After the event, the signed book would be in a small brown bag with their name on the outside in the entryway. They could take it when they left. It was better to work in the signings then; not everybody had the book or wanted to buy it. Picking up their book after the event would avoid bad feelings or regrets from other guests. Because he needed to leave right after the program, Congressman Obey signed the books before the event.

It all worked out better than I expected.

John, one of the Democratic Party staffers, was picking up the congressman at the Milwaukee airport. John was a good choice. He was dedicated to the party, had good manners, and would appreciate the drive with this legendary U.S. congressman. Having the opportunity to be with U.S. Congressman Obey was an honor for him. On that Friday evening, John phoned and said the congressman's flight had arrived.

An hour and a half later, John was at the door smiling, and so was the congressman. Our foodie volunteers were in the kitchen prepping the food for the following day's event. The congressman met the volunteers. They were thrilled to meet this well-known and respected man, especially in this relaxed atmosphere. We went upstairs and showed him the bedroom and bathroom. He wanted to rest. About an hour later, he came down and joined the volunteers and sat at the kitchen bar overseeing the food preparation. We fed him fresh veggies, and I had ground beef for a hamburger. One of the volunteers seized the opportunity to make his hamburger. He requested that it be medium to well done. He seemed to be comfortable and enjoyed the activity in the kitchen.

An hour later, the volunteers left, to return at eight the next morning to ready the food. The fundraiser was labeled a Farmers Market Brunch. It was to run from 10:30 a.m. to 12:30 p.m. We had forty-one sponsors and a full house, with nearly a hundred donors.

The $23,000 we took in was divided equally between the four state senator candidates. Everyone won.

Grouping several candidates together seemed like a good way to offer them support. We just always needed a well-known, respected headliner who would attract a good number of sponsors and attendees. It was also good for the candidates to meet each other. After the guests left, they could share and compare their experiences.

A few retired state legislators contacted me and let me know how difficult it was to fundraise in the northern part of Wisconsin. Its farming and tourism economies were unstable and seasonal. The districts were geographically large and sparsely populated. The Madison candidates would make calls asking for $100. Up north, the candidates could ask for only $25. People realized the disparity and were more willing to lend their support. The Madison Dems were always generous. When they learned about tough situations and why it might be proving especially difficult for a good candidate to win up north, they stepped up to the plate.

Being from a farming community in the middle of the state, I understood the conditions. But I was also determined to support women candidates from up north who were running for State Senate or Assembly seats. They were running for admirable reasons. There was no sense of entitlement or "It's my turn" comments. They had dynamic and carefully considered ideas for making their districts better. They wanted to fix broken state laws. They had done their homework before they decided to run. Some of the incumbent candidates were fighting desperately to hold on to their seats. I would find a date where four—sometimes five—candidates could be in Madison, and then I arranged a headliner.

My goal was for each candidate to take home $2,000 each. At the fundraiser, each woman candidate spoke from an index card about why they were running and their background, followed by questions from the guests.

Peg Lautenschlager was an ideal headliner. She was from the middle of the state and was the U.S. Attorney for the Western District of Wisconsin appointed by President Clinton. She was the state's first woman attorney general. Peg also served on the Attorney General's Advisory Committee under U.S. Attorney General Janet Reno. Peg was the first Wisconsinite ever to serve on the committee. She fought for public access to the

Wisconsin State Capitol during the protests of Act 10 and did pro bono legal work for young people in Fond du Lac. Many people knew and respected her. Peg was battling breast cancer while in office, yet she missed just a few workdays.

A few years later, her cancer had returned. She had to retire from the Wisconsin Ethics Commission. When I ran into her at a fundraiser for a women's group called Emerge in Milwaukee, I asked if she would be the headliner for a fundraiser at my home for several female candidates running for office from up north. Without hesitation, Peg said yes. I gave her some dates, and she called back the next day with two possibilities. I phoned the four candidates and asked them to work around Peg's dates. We figured out a date that worked for everyone.

It would be in early December. All the planning and calls went well. As expected, Peg was a terrific draw for the event. I checked in with her the night before to see how she was doing.

"The last couple of days were tough," she said in a hoarse voice. In the middle of our conversation, she had to leave the phone for a few minutes.

"Take your time, Peg."

I heard her coughing in the background. When she returned, I asked if she wanted to stay overnight at my house. After the planned event, her drive home would take an hour and a half. She said that spending the night would not be necessary. Two friends would be driving her. After I hung up, I wondered if she was going to make it to the fundraiser. She sounded weak on the phone.

The next day Peg arrived about twenty minutes early in a beautiful cream wool suit and a Santa's hat. She was energized. Our living room was full with eighty people.

Peg did something different at the end of her short talk. She expanded on a remark during my opening—we were short in reaching $2,000 per candidate. She walked the guests through the disparity and difficulty of fundraising up north. She described the savings of staff time that the $2,000 for each candidate would represent. She knew all the details from campaigning throughout the state during her run for state attorney general.

Her presentation resonated with the group. A couple of women wrote checks, and we reached $8,000 for the four candidates.

I called her the next day with the good news that we had reached our financial goal thanks to her compelling talk. I asked her to call me the next time she was in Madison so I could take her out for lunch. That was the last time I talked to Peg. She died ten weeks later. o

CHAPTER 9

A Mile-High Democratic National Convention

*"In the end, this is what this election is about:
Do we participate in a politics of cynicism
or a politics of hope?"*

–Barack Obama

In early April 2008, Michael O'Neil, the Midwest deputy finance director, called and invited me to the Obama campaign headquarters in downtown Chicago. It was a thank you for past and future fundraisers. I was thrilled at the prospect of seeing the offices and meeting the heroic core leaders organizing this unique campaign. It was an honor to be inside the Obama campaign.

Over the past months, there had been numerous articles in the media about the campaign and its "out of the box" culture and methods. At the time, the use of social media to influence voters was a political strategy that hadn't been used before. It was a bold decision on the part of the campaign. I expected the campaign directors had past successes that had given them the confidence to undertake this innovative plan of action.

Security was tight at the Prudential building in downtown Chicago, just across from Millennium Park. A number of security guards were posted at the registration desk, and Michael had to come down to the front entrance and sign for my security badge. Maybe this was just the process for an insurance building, or was it because of the campaign headquarters? I went through a turnstile to elevators that only stopped at designated floors—a common precautionary measure.

When we arrived at the office area, I noticed that all the office doors were left open—even David Axelrod's and Jim Messina's. After escorting me into their offices, Michael introduced me to both men. They knew my name and thanked me for my work. I was surprised and humbled by their kind words.

Nearly overwhelmed, I told them how much I enjoyed working on the fundraisers and was learning the makings of the political world at a fast pace. I told them how running my small stores on the University of Wisconsin campus had given me skills in dealing with people, making decisions on my feet, and taking calculated risks. I also let them know how much I liked the campaign mantras "No drama with Obama" and "Respect, empower, include." In these encouraging conversations, they exceeded my expectations.

I created a statewide activist group, Wisconsin Women for Obama, and months later, I brought eight of the women to Chicago for a headquarters tour. Again, David Axelrod's office door was open. I was surprised when one of the women excitedly just walked in to say hello.

I saw it happening from a distance and tried to stop her, but she was already inside. By the time I got to his door, she had already convinced him to come out and take a picture with all of us. I was relieved to see a big smile on his face, and he patiently waited as we gathered around him. A staffer took a picture. We all thanked Axe—as his staff called him.

I shared some words with him, and it seemed like he got a kick out of the episode.

But back to that first trip in early April. Michael wanted to talk to me about possibly being a delegate to the National Democratic Convention in Denver.

Another good part about this campaign was that its people never assumed that you should do something, or made you feel that you had to do something for the campaign. There were no orders, assumptions, or making you feel guilty. They seemed to understand and respect that volunteers might sometimes need to say "not now" or "no." This was truly a bottom-up culture—not a top-down way of doing things. I greatly appreciated this, and it may be why the campaign volunteer base grew so fast.

I told Michael that being on the National Finance Committee was enough. I was already anticipating the upcoming May meeting. I had discussed it on the phone with Katherine Gehl when she called and congratulated me on being asked to serve on the committee. She had already been to a couple of meetings and told me what to expect, which had gotten me even more excited.

I said to Michael that over the last three weeks, I had heard of many stressed Madison Dems jostling to be convention delegates. The state had a total of ninety-two Democratic slots. Many of those would be Hillary's delegates. (Hillary delegates felt similar stress and anxiety.) The committed Dems I knew were longtime party members. For them, going to their meetings was almost like going to church. I had not paid that much attention to the process since I wasn't considering attending the convention.

Michael said that the campaign was still a bit nervous that some Obama delegates were being persuaded to switch over to Hillary. Because of the amount of work I had done in the past six months, the campaign thought they could trust me to stand firm with Obama.

I understood his concern. I recalled the caucus in Iowa, where I saw people changing their minds at the last minute and voting for a different candidate. I checked my calendar for the convention dates: August 25 to 28. I was available.

I was intrigued by the idea of returning to Denver. Years earlier, I was there for a tour with city planners, who explained how they were developing their downtown. At the time, it was half empty storefronts, like most downtowns. The tour and their ideas for improving their city had been thoughtful and courageous. It would be interesting to see what they'd accomplished since then.

After taking note of my curiosity, suddenly he said, "You are a Democrat, aren't you?"

"What do you mean?"

"Don't you have a card?"

"A card? Why no. Do I need to have one?"

"Yes." He turned to his computer and Googled "Democratic Party of Wisconsin, being a delegate." After finding what he was looking for, he went to the printer. "Mary, it is important that you be a delegate. We trust you. Here is what you have to do." He handed me the printout.

There was a simple form for Democratic Party membership that had to be filled out and received at the party's office by April 18, along with a $25 check. Also, the printout stated that any interested members had to be present at two meetings, the first at the Dane County Dems meeting on Sunday, April 27 at the Labor Temple in Madison.

The second meeting would be at a high school in Verona, right outside of Madison. There the delegates would be confirmed for the Second Congressional District. There would be a roll call, and anybody's name that was not called had to show proof of their $25 membership payment. The roll call was a list from the county parties' elected delegates. The dates for the county and congressional district caucuses were just a few weeks away. I again checked my calendar. I was in town for both caucuses.

He gave me a stamped envelope and asked me to please get it in the mail first thing the next morning with my check.

Also, much to my surprise, Michael added that I would be receiving a signed letter from Senator Obama thanking me for what I had done for his campaign and stating that he wanted me to be one of his Wisconsin delegates.

The letter would prove to be very powerful; it had his signature. It was amazing to see that it was written personally to me. He talked about the fundraiser at my home on October 15, 2007, and thanked me for its success. The letter was on his personal campaign stationary.

A week later I received a letter welcoming me into the Democratic Party of Wisconsin signed by the chair, Joe Wineke. I would be at the Dane Dems County Party Caucus. At these events, each county registers its members, after which that number prorates each county. This part of a formula helps determine how many convention delegates each county and state can have.

There were two separate rooms that Sunday at the Madison Labor Temple: one for Hillary's supporters and the other for Obama's. I was in the Obama room, caucusing to people who would be voting for the delegate positions.

There were about fifty people in our group. Everyone was caucusing for themselves. Some members brought friends to campaign with them, while others had a support letter from the governor.

My daughter Muffy was my engaging and spirited campaigner. I was glad she came because it was difficult to talk about myself. It sounded too much like bragging. I spoke to the voting Dems about Senator Obama being at my home and the five fundraisers totaling $100,000 for the campaign. I also shared my support letter from Obama. Only one other person—a grassroots organizer—had a letter from the candidate.

After about an hour, the election started. My name was suggested first and went on the blackboard. Twelve more names went up. We each had to stand and say why we should be a delegate. We had just a few minutes.

I reiterated the same things I had said during the caucus and ended by holding up Obama's letter. The next person presented her case. Each of the names on the blackboard followed suit.

The voting started with my name, and I received a large number of votes. After that round, the people who were not in the top tier were eliminated.

I would be a "delegate at large." I was glad to be a delegate and follow through for Barack and Michael. I didn't want to let down either of them.

When I got home, I emailed the results to Michael. He was happy and relieved.

The Second Congressional District Caucus was a few weeks later in Verona. There were over a hundred people in the gym. It was understandable why there was anxiety about being a delegate. It was a historic convention where either the first woman or first black man would be the Democratic candidate running for the office of President of the United States.

The meeting started on time. After a few announcements, Joe Wineke, the chair of the Democratic Party of Wisconsin, went right to the roll call of the delegates. When he came to my name, he said, "This is a mistake. Where is Mary Lang Sollinger?"

I raised my hand.

He looked at me from the stage and said, "You're not a member." Joe had been the state chair for several years and was a former state legislator. He knew everyone in his district and many in the state.

Since this was new territory, I had planned for the worse but hoped for the best. I brought two copies of the cashed check and two copies of the welcome letter from the Democratic Party of Wisconsin (DPW). Joe's signature was handwritten on the letter. This was the caucus where the proof of membership was important.

I told him I had his DPW membership letter and copies of my cashed check. I started passing the copies through the seated audience.

Joe asked to see the letter. Someone in the audience took one of the copies to the stage. He looked at it, gave it back, and continued with the next name. None of the other names were questioned.

Being a woman and during my younger years in business, I was frequently questioned about why I was on this commission or that committee. Sometimes I was being tested. If I questioned an idea during a meeting, I was then asked an intimidating question. Rough experiences teach long-lasting lessons.

The next day, I booked a flight to Denver. We paid for our own flights and hotel rooms. The Democratic Party had sent out information about booking hotel rooms for the Wisconsin delegation. Luckily, our hotel was near the downtown convention center.

On Monday, August 25, I arrived in Denver in the morning. On a pleasant ride from the airport, the taxi driver excitedly talked about the convention and offered me coupons, mainly for restaurants and some museums. I had questions, and he had answers. He must have had training. It would make sense that the cab companies would have provided their drivers with extra guidelines and information for the thousands of delegates. Most likely, they would be the first people the conventioneers would engage with.

A number of Madison delegates were staying at the same hotel. My room was small, but fine for one person. Excited to see the new downtown, I quickly unpacked. I walked to Sixteenth Street, the main street, which has many passenger stops for their light rail system. That would drop me off just a half a block from the convention center.

The city planners had done a great job. Sixteenth Street had been updated with many Western and rugged mountain details. You sure knew you were in Denver. I went to pick up my Wisconsin credentials for the convention—one for Tuesday and another for Wednesday.

At the Pepsi Center convention hall, most of the planned speakers would be Democratic senators, U.S. members of Congress, and state governors. My credentials could also be used for workshops at the convention center, public transportation and shuttles, and special events like breakfasts with our legislators and members of Congress.

A third credential was for Invesco Field—sometimes called Mile High Stadium—on the convention's last day. That's when and where the nominated candidate would be making his or her acceptance speech as the Democratic candidate for president. Also in my bag were coupons for restaurants and stores, as well as some fun Colorado and Denver souvenirs.

From the Democratic National Committee emails I had received a few weeks earlier, I was told to pick up additional credentials because of the fundraising I had done for Candidate

Obama. Those credentials were for the National Finance Committee, located upstairs in the convention center. I was a "finance guest," which meant I was new and didn't have a track record of donating to the DNC, only to the presumed presidential candidate Barack Obama.

My finance guest credentials included special seating on the playing field for the last night at Invesco Field. When getting this packet of credentials, I asked if I could bring a guest to any of the events. The staff member apologized and said that there wasn't enough room in the venues. That was frustrating but understandable. Still, my heart was beating faster. I had invites to receptions and special seating opportunities for exciting events.

I had two hours for lunch. Even though it was the first morning of the convention, the mall and streets were busy. I remembered the shuttered storefronts from my previous trip to Denver. Now the stores had customers, and the restaurants' large staffs were preparing for busy lunches. It was great to see the rebirth of their downtown.

The first reception I planned to attend was for will.i.am from the Black Eyed Peas, held at the historic Brown Hotel just blocks from the convention center.

The Brown Hotel was breathtaking, transporting me back to a more opulent age. Overlooking an atrium of natural light were beautiful natural stone, handmade wrought iron railings for eight open floors. The stunning use of wood—presumably from the forests in the nearby Rocky Mountains—gave the entrance a semblance of strength, with hand labor by expert craftsmen.

How lucky I felt to be in this grand place to see a famous American rapper and songwriter. He had made an unusual and far-reaching contribution to the Obama campaign. Will.i.am had released two videos in February that swept the country: "We Are the Ones" and "Yes, We Can," both collages of all kinds of American citizens. Some were famous; most were not. Both videos urged people to vote.

I asked the hotel staff where the room was, and they led me to a room off the main entrance.

It was smaller than expected for someone who had made such an impact on the younger market. There were only about forty people in the room. Most of us were standing. I wished that I had brought something for will.i.am to sign.

The rapper entered, recognizing some people and going over to them. He had a nice ambiance and warm smile. He gave us a short talk about what had motivated him to produce the video for Obama. It was pure admiration for Candidate Obama, as well as respect for all those who had passed before—those whose struggle had made Obama's candidacy possible. Some questions followed, and then he had to go. It was over in about twenty minutes, and worth being there to see will.i.am in person and gain more of an understanding of his talent. I loved the videos. Feeling their message of inclusion had made an enormous difference.

I took the light rail on Sixteenth Street back to the hotel, hoping more Wisconsinites had arrived. They were there! Red Bucky Badger and Green Bay Packers shirts were suddenly everywhere. I ran into Madison friends, along with other friends from up north. They had just picked up their credentials.

We left together to get a shuttle to the Pepsi Center—too far away to walk. The lines at the designated shuttle pick-up stops were long. Fortunately, the buses were fast in loading and leaving. We grabbed any empty seat we could find.

The people in front of me were from MoveOn.org. They were easy to identify from their T-shirts. I started to tell them what an inspirational organization they had. They were endorsing Obama.

One of them was a high energy, engaging young woman named Ilyse, who was very excited and talkative. She was rallying the bus to chant, "Yes, we can!" After the chant ended, she and I talked about what Obama's presidency would mean for the country. When we were nearing the Pepsi Center, Ilyse gave me her business card. She had an impressive job position. She asked for my business card.

I should have known better after having business cards for over twenty-five years while I had my business. But it had not occurred to me to bring them to the convention. As life goes, three years later, Ilyse and I would meet again by happenstance in Washington, D.C., at a small dinner with Vice-President Joe Biden. By then, we had iPhones and easily exchanged our updated contact information.

I grabbed some food, then found the Wisconsin sign and section in the hall. High up in an elevated area, we had a full view of the stage and podium. It looked spectacular. Well-dressed people were pouring into the vast hall. Red, white, and blue banners; balloon arches; and lighting created a wonderful ambiance for the special and memorable day ahead. The music was upbeat, using many popular and current songs.

The theme of the day was "One Nation." Caroline Kennedy introduced a video titled "The Work to Come: A Tribute to Senator Edward Kennedy." Due to his illness, Senator Kennedy had not been expected to attend the convention, but that evening he made a surprise appearance and gave a short speech. Senator Kennedy was recuperating from brain surgery. He said, "For me this is a season of hope—new hope for a justice and fair prosperity for the many, and not just for the few—new hope." Senator Kennedy continued with, "Barack Obama will close the book on the old politics of race and gender and group against group and straight against gay. And Barack Obama will be a commander-in-chief who understands that young Americans in uniform must never be committed to a mistake, but always for a mission worthy of their bravery."

The audience gave the senator a standing ovation that lasted a few minutes. Many had tears in their eyes.

The program ended with a video about former President Jimmy Carter's inspiring humanitarian work with a focus on Habitat for Humanity, followed by a brief appearance by President Carter himself. The crowd gave him a standing ovation.

Throughout the day, there were over thirty speakers, all notable Democrats. I took notes on the program.

That evening Michelle Obama was the prime-time speaker. Her brother, Craig Robinson, introduced her. In her speech, she explained how her husband embraced the "One Nation" idea. "That's why Barack's running, to end the war in Iraq responsibly … to build an economy that lifts every family, to make sure healthcare is available for every American, and to make sure that every single child in this nation has a world-class education. He'll achieve these goals the same way he always has—by bringing us together and reminding us how much we share and how alike we really are. You see, Barack doesn't care where you're from or what your background is or what party, if any, you belong to." Powerful applause followed, with thousands of cheering Dems jumping to their feet and showing their full support.

It seemed that every time I went to the restroom or got something to eat, I spotted a famous person. One time, I literally knocked into Donna Brazile; I excused myself. She was very gracious, and I was tongue-tied. Another time, CNN contributor Roland Martin was sprinting through the back hallway, maybe late for an interview. The energy was high everywhere.

It was thrilling.

Tuesday began with breakfast at the hotel with U.S. Congressman Ron Kind, serving his sixth term as U.S. Congressman for the western part of Wisconsin. His wife and two young sons were with him. The congressman congratulated the room full of Wisconsin delegates for their work for the Democratic Party and reminisced about the great speakers of the night before.

After breakfast, some Madison delegates and I headed to the convention center for workshops.

Midday, before the program started, I used my finance guest credential to attend a reception with other DNC National Finance Committee members. This behind-the-scenes tour ended on stage, beside the podium where the convention speakers stood. It was a delight to be in the same spot where Michelle Obama, the Kennedys, and President Jimmy Carter had been the night before.

That evening's program started with Senator Barbara Mikulski on the podium. Congresswomen Nancy Pelosi and Governor Kathleen Sebelius were also among the thirty-plus speakers. I was able to meet Governor Sebelius when she had been in Madison, so it was exciting to see her on the podium and to hear why she was supporting Barack Obama.

I was very impressed by Lilly Ledbetter's speech about pay equity. After nineteen years at Goodyear, Lilly had received an anonymous note revealing that she was making thousands less per year than the men in her same position. Devastated, she filed a sex discrimination case against Goodyear, which she won—and then heartbreakingly lost on appeal.

Later on, I kept an eye out for her and eventually got lucky. I went over to meet her in the back hallway as she was leaving a group of admirers. It was perfect timing to thank her for coming forward with her case. I asked what had made her decide to speak out.

She said it had been the moment when she found the note in her locker about the years of pay disparity. She'd finally had it and decided to do something about it. In 2012, I immediately bought her book *Grace and Grit* when it was released. A year later, I had the honor of doing a fundraiser with her as the headliner in Madison.

Later, the first bill President Obama signed was The Lilly Ledbetter Fair Pay Act of 2009, which bolstered worker protections against pay discrimination. I think that President

Obama fully understood the importance of this bill because of his grandmother's experience at the bank, where she kept training young men for their path to executive positions, while she was never promoted.

The convention headliner that night was Senator Hillary Clinton, introduced by her daughter Chelsea. The delegates gave Hillary a heartwarming standing ovation lasting at least four minutes. In her speech, Hillary opened up about "being a proud supporter of Barack Obama" and continued with, "We are on the same team." She said, "The time to unite is now. None of us can sit on the sidelines." After her speech, there was another monumental applause. I had enormous respect for Hillary. The next day, Wednesday, during the roll call, she would make the motion to officially nominate Senator Barack Obama by acclamation.

Ohio Representative Dennis Kucinich, who also ran as a presidential candidate in the 2008 Democratic Party primaries, gave a spirited speech. Structured around the refrain "Wake up America," it included criticism of the abuses of power of the current Bush/Cheney administration, as well as attacks on the corporate control of American politics. He explored social issues like universal healthcare. His words electrified the audience, who continued cheering his speech long after its ending.

Wednesday's theme for the day was "Securing America's Future" and featured a speech by the vice-presidential candidate and Senator Joe Biden. Senator Biden engaged the entire audience with his "down-home," sincere talk. He focused on Barack Obama's nomination and what kind of hope and change our country would have if Senator Obama would be president,

It was a truly memorable surprise seeing and hearing former presidential candidate John Kerry speak that day. He had a different persona, far different from the stiff candidate I remembered when he had been campaigning in Madison. Now he was relaxed, smiling, and weaving funny jokes into his speech.

I looked at the two Madison delegates in front of me and the three on one side of me. We all shed tears of disbelief, wondering where this genuine-feeling person had been during the 2004 campaign. Back then, just a few weeks before Election Day, Senator Kerry had come to Madison with Bruce Springsteen. A major downtown street near campus had been closed off to accommodate the 80,000 people who came to see "The Boss" and the candidate for president.

It had been a get-out-the-vote event. If back then Kerry had been the person he was that night at the Pepsi Center, he could have won the election. People want authenticity. In that election, candidates from both parties had been "handled" too much, with carefully scripted speeches written by staffs and consultants who were guided by polls. The candidates lost their personalities and their authenticity. With an Obama/Biden ticket, things would be different.

On, the convention's last day was at the Invesco Field/Mile High Stadium, a sports arena used mostly for the Denver Broncos. It was open to the elements. I hoped the weather stayed good. Happily, it was perfect that morning.

With my finance guest credential, I was able to go to a DNC National Finance Committee brunch. There was a shuttle from downtown to the restaurant, which was close to the stadium.

I found myself in a place where I didn't know anyone. Very few people were by themselves like me. As I scanned the large, noisy room, everyone looked appealing and interesting. As I slowly moved through the crowd, I decided just to start talking to anyone else I spotted who was also alone.

I started talking to a young man about the historic evening coming up. Like me, he was from the Midwest—Chicago. It was good to share common ground. We discussed the chances of Obama and Biden winning in November, both of us cautiously optimistic.

After ten minutes, he asked my name. I just said, "Mary."

His was Jesse. I looked at him again carefully, with a soft, questioning smile. "Jesse Jackson's son?"

With a wide smile, he looked a bit surprised at the recognition.

"Holy smokes," I said. "What an honor." I read in a recent article that Jesse Jackson Sr. was still holding out his support for Obama, even though his son was a national co-chair of the Obama campaign. The younger Jesse was trying to persuade his father to come on board with Obama.

We talked a bit more before someone came over wanting to talk to Jesse. I had planned to meet some Wisconsin delegates in the stadium and left, wishing him the best.

The Democratic National Campaign Committee had a record crowd of more than 84,000 people in attendance. Eight thousand conventioneers were on the playing field, and the other 76,000 would be roaring in the stands in a few hours.

I arrived a little late at the entrance where we had planned to meet and only saw Wisconsin delegates Roberta, Stan, and

Jordan. Everyone else was in the stadium. The Wisconsin delegation was in the stands. We were told to go early to get a good seat.

Thanks again to the finance guest credential, I was in a small group of Wisconsin Dems on the playing field nearer the stage. Governor Doyle and his wife, Jessica; some of his cabinet members; the superdelegates; and I would be sitting in this section. We were about thirty feet from the curtained four-foot barrier for the large staging area and podium. The stage was raised five to six feet. The Wisconsin VIP section would be able to see the speakers and the show from our chairs on the field.

It turned out that we had plenty of time to find our seats. They were testing the sound systems and screens. Security was doing another sweep for anything suspicious. It was fascinating to see the number of people and coordination needed to carry off a massive production like this.

I sat in our Wisconsin area and met the superdelegates from up north and Milwaukee. A young man named Milt came and took a seat next to Christine, a friend of mine from up north. This was Milt's second convention. We three had a lot to discuss. We talked about some of the memorable events of the last three days. Milt was concerned about a rumor of protesters and security issues.

All three of us noticed how strange it was seeing the TV stations in the Pepsi Center—CNN, MSNBC, CBS, and ABC—elevated in what Wisconsin hunters would call "deer stands." Reporters were located inside these basic huts, which—unlike deer stands—were surrounded by glass. They were about twenty feet above the conventioneers and main floor. Their support crews were on the main floor and hardly seen, but they were always available when needed.

Our Wisconsin delegation seats were higher than they were. We could see inside because of the large glass windows. The reporters didn't react to any sight or sound outside of the hut and rarely looked outside. Once in a while, they must have looked at the stage, but none of us ever saw that happen. They were on laptops, in their own world. The symbolism of their setup was not missed. The stadium was filling with people of every color and variety. There were the young and old. People in wheelchairs. Some were dressed for the warm day. Others wore dresses, suits, or colorful ethnic attire. I saw people in cowboy hats and others in their Sunday hats.

From the crowd, I heard my name being called.

"Hey, Mary!"

I spotted John Imes. Back in October 2007 for Senator Obama's fundraiser at my home, John was one of the very few donors I didn't have to call up and ask for a donation. After receiving the invitation, he automatically signed up online. I remember that he asked if he could bring his two oldest children, Jack and Cora, for the photo op with the candidate.

"Of course," I said, happy to have the next generation present.

But in Denver, I knew John wasn't a delegate, so I was surprised to see him. I called him over and asked him how in the world he managed to get in.

When the DNC Convention was announced in 2008, John had to get creative and do some research to be able to attend his first convention. John was the executive director of Wisconsin

Environmental Initiative, a nonprofit he co-founded in 1996 that advocates for green building, development, and clean water. As a member of Obama's Energy & Environment (E&E) Policy Team, John wanted to get to the Denver convention and connect with fellow E&E team members whom he knew would be there.

But first, he needed to find a place to stay. Hotel rooms were scarce and prohibitively expensive; rentals like Airbnb were unavailable. He went on Craigslist, and after days of searching, he stumbled across a listing for a condo located at the RiverClay, the Rocky Mountain region's first green-certified residential development. John called, but the location was booked up.

John got bold and called the RiverClay developer and said he wanted to showcase RiverClay to his fellow members of the Obama campaign E&E Policy Team. To the developer's credit, he not only offered their model green condo to the group but offered it as their meeting place as well.

Two weeks later, John flew out. RiverClay had an opportunity to meet and discuss their project with the E&E group. John ended up on an air mattress in the manager's condo. The developer donated the generous rate of $50 rate per night, for four nights, to the Obama campaign.

John began each day of the convention at the hotel where the Wisconsin delegation breakfasted every morning. He was able to secure credentials for each night plus tickets to special events. There were clean tech and green business round tables, campaign briefings and film sneak previews, bipartisan receptions and clean energy demonstrations.

And on that final, incredible, historic night at Invesco Field, John was grateful to be among the 84,000 people on hand when Barack Obama gave his nomination speech as the Democratic candidate for president. John proceeded to find a seat in the Wisconsin delegation in the stands.

It looked like the entire country was going to play a part in this memorable evening. It was reassuring and made me feel like "We Are the Ones" and "Yes, We Can." The program started with popular singer Sheryl Crow followed by the amazing Stevie Wonder. I enjoyed will.i.am and John Legend singing together with the Agape International Choir.

Under a clear and starry night, speakers included former Vice President Al Gore, Governor Tim Kaine of Virginia, Governor Bill Richardson of New Mexico, and Illinois Senator Dick Durbin.

When Barack Obama entered the stage, he was greeted with a long and resounding applause. It took several minutes before the crowd settled down. He reminded us that "Our government should work for us, not against us. It should ensure opportunity, not just for those with the most money and influence, but for every American who is willing to work. That's the promise of America, the idea that we are responsible for ourselves, but that we also rise and fall as one nation, and the fundamental belief that I am my brother's keeper, I am my sister's keeper. That's the promise we need to keep, that's the change we need right now."

Michelle, Malia, Sasha, Joe and Jill Biden joined Candidate Obama on the stage. The long thunderous applause was then absorbed by enormous fireworks encircling the stadium.

Confetti blew over the stage. The young Obama girls loved it. I was amazed by how comfortable, reassured, and happy they were. It reflected what good parents both Barack and Michelle were.

Many conventioneers—both men and women—were crying tears of joy. No one was in any hurry to leave. It was like everyone wanted to freeze this moment in time in their hearts and memory. But eventually, we all parted and hoped to see each other again.

More than thirty-eight million people across ten U.S. cable and broadcast TV networks tuned in to witness history. After being so incredibly inspired and motivated that night, I could only hope that all those viewers watching from home felt the same—not only to vote for Obama but to get involved right away and work for the election of Obama and Biden.

For John, those three days of networking and making contacts were important for the meaningful work that lay ahead for him in Madison.

A few months later, when Barack Obama was president, a "National House Party Day to Re-energize America" event was organized. The national event included thousands of guests at 220 house parties in all fifty states engaged in a national conversation on green jobs, clean technology, climate change, and energy independence. Participants represented the political, business, and activist spectrums.

John organized the National House Night at the Orpheum Theater in downtown Madison, which seats over one thousand. The program consisted of remarks from President Barack Obama and a national live teleconference with former Vice

President Al Gore, where he addressed John's question about ways "we might better engage mainstream corporations and Main Street businesses." Later, John was empowered to run successfully for local office and continues to serve on municipal commissions.

With experience in the hospitality business and his boundless energy, John also had been a great help at many of my fundraisers through the years. That historic day in Denver, when we accidentally saw each other at Mile High Stadium, we agreed that politics as usual is no longer an option.

We both had the good fortune to work inside the Obama culture where putting our state and country was first and foremost. We returned to Madison energized, promising that we would be involved and do all we could to elect Barack Obama over the nine weeks left before the November election. **O**

CHAPTER 10
Our Win

"Yes, we can!" ["Si, se puede!"]
—Cesar Chavez, United Farm Workers,
and adapted by will.i.am

There were ten more days before Tuesday, November 8.

Miles and Laura were smart, dedicated workers for Obama. Hans and I had been housing them for the last three months of the campaign. Miles was in charge of the University of Wisconsin campus area with its staple 38,000 undergraduate and graduate student population. Laura was responsible for the greater west side area of Madison. When they returned to our home after one of their very many long days, I realized that since my Obama fundraisers in Madison were done, I was now able to help them out.

During the long campaign, some campaign workers had become rundown and sleep-deprived. I asked if they needed help canvassing or making calls. Miles said they did. His campus office had a list of phone numbers that needed to be called, to remind the students when and where to vote on Election Day.

Laura received several recognitions for her phenomenal organizing successes. She had personally made the most phone calls in the nation to voters to inspire them to get out and vote. Her team was one of the top producers in the country for getting out the vote. There was no doubt in anyone's mind that she deserved her many honors.

The next day, I went to the campus office, and Miles gave me several pages of student phone numbers to call. I stayed on the phones that day and the next. On the third day, Heidi called from the office in the southeast part of Madison and asked if I would join her. She was just transferred there, and they needed help.

The volunteers in her office were slowing down from exhaustion and nonstop canvassing, making calls, and driving teams to their turfs for the past several weeks. Many were working full-time and came in after work and on weekends. Some were older retirees.

I checked with Miles, and he said the calls were under control at his office. They were covered through Election Day, just six days away. He thanked me for my three days of work, and the following day I moved to Heidi's office. After that, we worked eight to ten hours a day. The time flew by. This was our last chance to help Senator Barack Obama win.

I was torn about whether I should go to Chicago's Millennium Park the night of the election, where we hoped Obama would be speaking as the new president of the country, or stay in Madison and continue canvassing until the polls closed. I chose to stay in Madison because I wanted to be with the donors and volunteers like Heidi who had supported the fundraisers and who canvassed and got out the vote.

She and I would await the election results in the exhibition hall at the Monona Terrace, where Barack had the rally before he came to my house in October. The Madison Obama events were coming full circle.

Heidi and I met at the Monona Terrace around 9 p.m. after the Madison polls closed. The Rocky Mountain states and the West Coast polls would be open for another two hours.

Many of us were exhausted and hoped it wouldn't be a long night. We were nervous and tired. We started to reminisce about all the things we did together for Barack Obama's campaign. Heidi had been there since day one when I first received the call about hosting Senator Obama. At this pivotal moment, I asked her what had motivated her to get so involved.

Heidi was born and raised in Munich, Germany, and had come to the United States on a scholarship to Lawrence University in Appleton, Wisconsin. That's where she met her former husband. Through him, she was introduced to his grandfather, who for twenty-four years, had been a U.S. senator for Wisconsin.

The American political process intrigued Heidi, and while making a life here with her children, she had learned all she could about this country's political structure and the importance of citizenship input. Being born in Germany during World War II, she'd seen firsthand the evil that followed when good people did nothing. Heidi was determined not to let history repeat itself in her adopted country. She proudly became a citizen in 1983. She firmly believed in the promise and reality of America.

She told me that she was so excited to see Senator Obama. In Heidi's words, "I developed previously unknown powers of persuasion as I called friends and former colleagues for sizable contributions to Candidate Obama's campaign." Heidi helped out with many of the fundraiser preparations. She said it was one of the most important moments of her life when Senator Obama stepped into my living room. Heidi loved how he had energized the assembled citizens, answering people's questions, and even taking pictures with the volunteers.

Heidi continued to work on getting out the vote by standing at intersections holding large "Vote for Obama" signs in downtown Dubuque in freezing weather, knocking on hundreds of doors in Madison, and helping me with five more fundraisers and making calls on Election Day. It was hard to believe that she was sixty-seven years old.

CNN was on big screens. Renee and Bruce, who had been with me at Pittsburgh, also joined us. We all started to think about what would happen if Obama lost the election. What would our country look like in the future? The economy would be in jeopardy, the housing collapse would continue, the banks would have more failures and, even worse, we could be starting another war.

All of a sudden it got very quiet. All eyes were on the large screens. CNN called the win for Obama before the California and Washington polls were closed. Barack Obama, now *President* Obama, had 52.9 percent of the vote.

Nearly four thousand supporters exploded with tears and hugs of pure joy. Heidi and I stayed to watch President Obama give his celebration speech at Millennium Park, with thousands of cheering supporters and media cameras from all over the world.

I thought of the old gray-haired woman in Indianapolis and her prophecy of how badly Obama would be treated in Washington, D.C., if he won. I hoped she would see his strong margin of victory and feel better. *He was going to be fine,* I told myself.

Exhaustion soon hit. Friends and volunteers left for home. At 12:15 a.m., Senator John McCain conceded to the new president.

The next morning, I slept in late and woke up still half asleep. Was the win true, or had I just dreamt it?

I went outside to get the newspaper. It was great to see the headline: "A New Dawn." There it was. It really did happen. All the tireless days, exhausting nights, and exhilarating experiences were worth it. Millions of Americans made history for our country and for the world too.

We can do it again. **O**

CHAPTER 11

What I Learned: Respect, Empower, Include

*"I don't like that man. I have to
get to know him better."*

—Abraham Lincoln

In *Dreams from My Father*, both Obama's search to find his destiny and his prioritization of values resonate throughout. Barack Obama was an exceptional presidential candidate, perhaps an anomaly.

Most of his life, he was in uncommon situations. He didn't have a father. After living in Jakarta when he was young, he returned to the U.S. to attend a distinguished prep school in Hawaii. He lived with his maternal grandparents during his formative years and experienced a liberal arts college founded by the Presbyterian clergy, then finished his education at Columbia and Harvard, both prestigious universities. All those transitions were monumental. All played a part in who he became.

I recall the lines from Robert Frost's poem: "I took the one less traveled by, and that made all the difference." To take that less-traveled road, Obama must have had deep curiosity and confidence. This unusual road took him to higher truths and aspirations that he shared with our country. He developed an uncanny but clear scope of right and wrong. It gave him self-assurance. He reminded me of a quote my father would say: "If you are doing the right thing, things will work out."

If you haven't already, I urge you to read *Dreams from My Father* and draw your own conclusions. It was written in 1995, right after he graduated from Harvard. It was long before he entered the political world.

Barack Obama was the first president that had extensive and successful community organizing experience, including fundraising. With this grassroots foundation, he had a full understanding of the power of a well-directed staff and the importance of volunteers. That can make all the difference. He brought a new culture to politics.

It was the antithesis to the traditional political culture of politics, which included the following: pulling your opponent through the mud on personal issues, double-talking on issues

- not respecting volunteers
- top-down decision making
- over-handling of candidates in public venues where their personalities are camouflaged over-rehearsed "stump" speeches

- not engaging at events and fundraisers by not taking questions from the donors and supporters
- supporting candidates who are running for self-interested or egotistical reasons rather than valued-base motivations to better their state or country

Republicans like Sarah Palin derided Obama's community organizing because its selfless motives were difficult for them to understand. What they didn't get about these experiences is what made Barack Obama such an outstanding candidate. I think that if other politicians had similar community experiences, no doubt our politics would be different and have a different moral compass today.

Obama's personal history, his short list of political experience, and his African name would not predict a bid, much less a win for the country's highest office. But through the years, Obama had developed long-term relationships with community and business leaders of integrity, trust, and pragmatism.

He brought with him a new kind of politics, one filled with sincerity, engagement, and authenticity. I believe that his 2008–2012 campaign mantra of respect, empower, include—all action words—was one of the main reasons he won in 2008.

Amazingly, I never heard a disgruntled staffer or volunteer in the Obama campaign offices. After thinking long and hard, I cannot recall a volunteer leaving the campaigns. At times they needed a time-out, usually from exhaustion, but they would return. In fact, many would continue with their OFA (Obama for America) teams after the election. They converted to a new OFA (Organizing for America), which focused on issues like voter suppression and healthcare. Ten years later, some Wisconsin team leaders like Claudia Pogreba and Ann Muenster continue having town hall meetings in which they address voter protection and other current issues.

In both the 2008 and 2012 campaigns, there was no behind-the-scenes volleying for prestige tasks, like driving the candidate and maybe getting a photo. There was no talk about working there to build a resume and no planning about what kind of job was desired in the White House. There was only talk of working to better our state and country.

On that first day of canvassing in Dubuque, Iowa, for the primary, I heard "respect, empower, include" from Michael Dorsey, Obama's field organizer.

Those three simple words went straight to my backbone. Throughout the day, they echoed in my head. Those words felt good and they settled conflicts.

When in doubt, respect, empower, and include. It's so simple. When someone you meet says something confusing or just wrong, respect them; don't prejudge them. Listen to what they mean. Ask a question or find something kind to say. Be agreeable. This strategy made our campaign door knocking less confrontational and more of a greeting. It was easier to give a reassuring smile. It made everything less stressful and empowered me to continue knocking on doors even longer.

When I returned to the Dubuque campaign office that day, I noticed all the "Respect, Empower, Include" signs in different formats and colors on the walls. The staff and volunteers had shared their own interpretations of these three words. They became the mantra for field organizers and teams after that

2008 Iowa primary win. Every field office I went to in Wisconsin, Indianapolis, and Pittsburgh had REI signs on their walls.

Respect, empower, include still resonates today. Recently, when I heard Felesia Martin talk to a group of Wisconsin Democratic women, she emphasized the importance of respecting other's concerns and issues when knocking on doors or in conversations at events. After that, engage—once knowing what's important to them and what's in their hearts. We must demonstrate true caring and concern for people, replacing scripted talking points with an authentic interest for what people are facing and going through daily.

Felesia is a former Republican who became a volunteer team leader and trainer for the 2008 Obama campaign. She did anything that was needed—from loaning her car to providing food for volunteers working late-night hours to making sure the copy machine always had paper. Felesia is now the Democratic Party of Wisconsin (DPW) 1st Vice-Chair.

Ben Wikler took respect, empower, and include to a different level when he ran for the DPW chair. Ben wanted to resurrect REI for his campaign slogan: FIRE—Fight, Include, Respect, Empower. He had a landslide win.

When I went into the world of politics, mentoring interns came easily and was rewarding. I felt I was making a difference. The mentoring continued in my volunteer work for Obama's fundraising events and giving talks to various political organizations.

One of the mentees was Steve Olikara. He used respect, empower, include to help make a dream come true. We met through Bryon Eagon while working on Zach Brandon's campaign for Dane County executive. A drive together to Milwaukee for a political event sealed our long-term friendship.

I often received invitations for political events in Milwaukee and would share my invitations with folks from my list of Obama supporters. Students, as well as donors, were on this list. Sometimes students wanted to attend these events as volunteers but didn't have a car. Then I'd receive a call from them needing a ride.

I got a call like this from Steve. He was a junior at the University at the time, a son of immigrants from India, doing well in school, and was intrigued with politics, although he or his parents had no previous interest or experience in the political world. Still, I could tell his parents had instilled pride in Steve about being an American.

Driving back to Madison after a political event in Milwaukee, he shared a dream, a hope. Steve had noticed how deadlocked things were in our State Capitol and Washington, D.C. He felt something should be done, that this was something his generation should be able to fix. He wanted to start a bipartisan group of millennials who were running for office and who were studying to be policymakers in both the Democratic and Republican Parties. He thought personal relationships would develop during their studies, campaigns, and would continue after they won seats in the U.S. Congress.

The drive was an hour and a half. We had good dialogue. I was supportive and asked thought-provoking "what ifs" and "whys." He already had a name: Millennial Action Project.

We stayed in contact and would occasionally meet for a cup

of coffee. We would always discuss his bold idea of bipartisan relationships and his dream of starting an organization.

His senior graduation came, and I was thrilled to see Steve as the president of his class giving the commencement speech. Also, I was happy to meet his parents at his graduation party and tell them what an exceptional son they had. They too were surprised at how Steve's self-confidence had grown these last few years.

With a developed and hard-thought-out business plan for Millennial Action Project (MAP), he went to Washington, D.C., with youthful optimism and enthusiasm.

During my trips to Washington as a National Finance Committee member for President Obama and later for the DNC, Steve and I would connect for coffee or lunch. I saw his small, rented, one-person office for MAP grow to become the largest nonpartisan organization of young lawmakers in the U.S. It worked with over eight hundred policymakers in Congress and state legislatures. MAP continues to build the next generation of leadership to rise above the partisan divide, to strengthen our democracy. Steve has become a nationally recognized political commentator for many media outlets.

When he was in Madison for a board meeting for the University, we had time for dinner. I told him about the progress while writing this book. In 2018, he co-authored a book on John F. Kennedy, and I was looking for some tips. He wanted to know why I was writing the book. Steve is a great listener. I told him how then-Senator Obama had enriched my life. It was a strange thing to say at my age—I am old enough to buy senior tickets at the movie theater—but it was true.

Although our backgrounds are very different, Steve and I have a few things in common. We both are somewhat shy, but both of us wanted more in our lives. We wanted to give more to the people around us. We both felt a deep loyalty to our country.

I asked him about what had made the difference for him.

Steve received a call in September 2010 from his good friend and organizer, J.D. Stier, telling him to meet him at Library Mall on the University of Wisconsin–Madison campus. J.D. was working at the White House at the time.

When Steve arrived, J.D. asked him, "Do you know that Obama is going to speak here on campus?"

Steve had heard rumors. They continued walking around Library Mall, where the rally was planned, discussing Wisconsin's importance in the election and how President Obama's visit would help rally volunteers and organizers.

J.D. said to Steve, "The president's point person for Wisconsin is looking for the right speakers with authentic Wisconsin voices." He looked at Steve and asked, "What would you think about emceeing the rally?"

Steve was stunned. He knew Madisonians would turn out in droves for the president. It could potentially be Obama's largest audience since taking office. "Of course, I would be happy to."

J.D. loved giving people an opportunity, especially those like Steve who didn't come from a background of political privilege. Respect, empower, include were ingrained in both of them.

But it wasn't a done deal. J.D. had to submit Steve's name and information to Obama's state director and the White House to be vetted. And there might be other names in consideration as well. He told Steve to expect a phone call in the next day or so.

A day passed. Then another. Three or four days passed.

Eventually, it was just a couple of days before the rally. Steve started to think the phone call wasn't coming. But he got a call from an unidentified number while he was at dinner.

"It still feels like yesterday," Steve said.

Dan Grandone, Obama's main point person for the state of Wisconsin, was on the phone. "We've heard a lot about you. We would love for you to emcee the rally on Tuesday. What do you think?"

Although he was concerned about the tight turnaround with the rally only a couple of days away, he thought it would all work out. Steve didn't change his mind.

Dan updated him on who would be speaking, including Congresswoman Tammy Baldwin and Senator Russ Feingold. The two musical acts Ben Harper and The National were performing. A rehearsal would be held the morning of the rally.

Steve called his mom and let her know the news. His dad was visiting family in India. With his mom by herself, Steve was concerned about her coming to the rally. She had never been to a political rally or a large concert. He urged her not to attend the rally but to watch it on the evening news in Milwaukee. He focused on his speech and decided on the fundamental idea, believing that we "ordinary people can do extraordinary things" for our country.

The day before the rally, Steve started to get information on how the stage would look. When it came to what to wear, the political staff said, "The president will be dressed business casual, no jacket. You don't want to out-dress the president, so make sure not to wear a jacket." The president and his staff knew the campus crowd.

There were massive preparations at Library Mall on the UW–Madison campus. The rally would be on the stairs of the library at one end of the State Street Mall.

Rally Day arrived. As Steve recalled, he showed up for rehearsal and saw musician Ben Harper just finishing up. The stage was huge. The setting looked beautiful.

When Steve stepped on stage, they brought out the presidential podium and asked him to stand behind it. A staffer told him, "Only the president is allowed to touch the podium. You cannot touch it." Steve never touched it.

Standing behind the podium at rehearsal, Steve thought, *This is either going to work out really well or really badly. Either I will freeze up, or I will discover that I can trust my voice.* His goal was to make his voice heard by the large crowd and to connect with them.

Steve huddled with Dan Grandone and his colleague Meagan Gardner at the Wisconsin Historical Society on the other end of Library Mall to discuss his remarks.

"Show us what you've got," they said.

Steve started to speak.

"No, louder!" Dan said, "as if thousands of people are in front of the stage." Periodically, Steve would glance down at his notes.

"No notes!" said Meagan. "You need to memorize your lines. We need you looking up from the podium. Your job is to get tens of thousands of people fired up before President Obama comes out. We'll stay here as long as you need to make sure you won't need notes."

Steve had given a few speeches on campus. But this was a test on a completely different scale. He took a deep breath, not knowing how he could memorize everything.

But the experience taught Steve to trust himself. As he was instructed by Dan, "Just speak from the heart. Trust your voice."

After running through his introduction a few times, he was due to rehearse on the stage, and he stood at the podium. He had to yell into the microphone.

"Just go for it!" Meghan yelled. "Give us the full volume, like you're introducing the president."

At this moment, they were still hours away from the rally.

Students were walking by on State Street, heading to class or to a cafe to study.

At first, he got nervous, but there was no turning back. He just had to do it.

Steve let those voices in his head go, and he let it rip. He gave them his opening at full volume.

People nearby looked over.

It felt good—what a relief.

When it was time, Steve lined up at the white security tent for presidential events. By then, he saw on social media that the crowd lining up to enter Library Mall was over a mile long, stretching across the entire campus. Many more people lined up than could possibly fit in State Street and Library Mall. (They later opened Bascom Hill, two blocks away, to accommodate the overflow.) The bands were readying to perform on stage and entertain the huge crowd.

Backstage, Steve met Steve Kerrigan from the White House advance team accompanying the president.

Steve K. told him he was "the voice of God," and he would introduce him. He brought Steve to a separate area to answer a few rapid-fire questions.

"Are you Steve Olikara?"

"Yes."

"Are you a proud Badger?"

"Yes."

When Steve K. later introduced Steve O., he would say, "And now please welcome to the stage a proud Badger, Steve Olikara!" That was Steve's cue to go to the podium.

Finally, it was rally time. Steve saw over 26,500 people outside, and there were many beyond his view. Just before heading outside, Steve saw David Axelrod, the president's White House senior advisor, on his phone. At that moment, Steve got a chill and remembered the sense of responsibility he had.

He filed onto the stage, and he was sitting next to State Senator Lena Taylor from Milwaukee. While looking out at the audience, she said, "I think someone wants to say hi to you." Steve saw his mother in the front row, standing next to a close family friend. Steve's mom was not going to miss this moment.

She held up her camera and took a picture of him.

It meant a lot for Steve to see her there. This path he was on felt so new and uncharted. He grew up as the son of Indian immigrants. His family had no clear playbook of how to get involved in politics. The Madison rally reaffirmed to Steve (and perhaps his mom) the possibilities of what America can offer people like his family.

When Steve O. heard Steve K., the voice of God, he walked to the podium. Steve O. felt ready and confident.

After a "Hello, Madison!" he launched into the speech. His voice came through as he spoke about why he was involved and why everyone should be involved in the upcoming election. In his speech, Steve spoke about a "different brand of politics. One built on hope, not fear. A vision and agenda not about scoring political points, but about solving our nation's toughest challenges that we've been putting off for years." He spoke of how Obama believed in young people to rebuild America. As Steve spoke, his voice echoed and reverberated farther than he could imagine. People were fired up.

After the rally, Steve O. and his close friends, along with Steve K. and his staff, went to State Street Brats to celebrate. As Steve recalled, "We sat on the patio. People walked by us, cheering and waving their hands. We watched the local news on TV that covered the rally. The realization of what the rally meant to people started to sink in."

Steve offered a final thought: "That night, as I reflected on all the excitement, I realized that I could trust my voice—and that it could connect with people on a deeper and broader level." That realization made the difference for him, determining what he could and would do in the future. **O**

CHAPTER 12

My Parents, My Hometown, Madison, and the School that Saved Me

"Common looking people are the best in the world; that is the reason why God made so many of them."

—Abraham Lincoln

Like many others I know, I sometimes wonder, "With a Republican dad, how in the world did I get from there to here?" Although politics was not a topic Dad ever discussed with us at the dinner table, during election cycles when I was growing up, our front yard in Campbellsport was crowded with Republican candidates' signs.

After moving to Madison, I was grateful to live in an internationally known university town. But I also occasionally wondered why my dad, a handsome, charismatic, and intelligent man, had chosen to settle in a small town. It never really made sense to me.

It could be that he was just more comfortable there. My mother said that World War II had made him tired. Post-traumatic stress syndrome had not been identified yet. I wondered if the silence and pride of that generation—what Tom Brokaw called "The Greatest Generation"—was a cover for trying to work things out while creating a more manageable post-war life. Dad had been "on the ground." He had witnessed tragedies up close, many involving innocent civilians, as well as soldiers on both sides.

My dad, Leo Lang, grew up on a dairy farm. Later, in Campbellsport, a village surrounded by farms and fifteen miles south of Fond du Lac, he spent thirty-two years as a teacher, principal, and school superintendent. The high school auditorium is named in his honor.

The farm where he grew up was in Marathon County, a little more than two hours north of Madison. He was part of a large family with eleven siblings. In those days, some families had that many children because they were Catholics; others had them because they needed help with the endless chores required on a farm. Both were the case with the Langs.

"We milked cows," my dad told author Lowell Peterson in an interview for Peterson's book, *The Sun Rose Clear: Stories of World War II and the Holocaust*. "[We] hatched thirty-six hundred chicks every year, sold eggs to Milwaukee hotels, and ran a cheese factory. We also had a blacksmith shop and ran a sawmill and a well-drilling machine." Brothers and sisters all pitched in. Getting the job done was dependent on the strength of their backs and arms. All their endeavors were sources of income for the large family. In winter months, Leo's dad, my grandfather, would head to the northern woods to work in lumberjack camps.

Graduating from high school in 1933, valedictorian of his class, Leo attended Central State Teachers College in Stevens Point, where he met my mother, LaNore Oleson. She was raised on a small farm near Mosinee, also in Marathon County. Even though they grew up only thirteen miles apart, they had never met before. LaNore was studying social science and home economics.

My dad went on for a master's degree in philosophy in education at the University of Wisconsin–Madison. His graduation ceremony was set for June 21, 1941, in Madison. If graduates wanted to receive their diploma, they were required to attend. Dad had been drafted into the United States Army, and induction day was June 18. On June 21, he had to be at Camp Wolters, Texas.

The graduation in Madison went smoothly by substituting my dad's brother Hizzie to walk across the stage when Leo Lang's name was called. Hizzie was smiling as he received the diploma and shook hands with the governor. Hizzie later admitted that before he walked on the stage, he was sweating, hoping that no one would notice he wasn't who he said he was—and if they did, that they wouldn't say anything.

LaNore joined Leo in Texas, and they were married in December 1941. My dad learned Morse code in the infantry communications school and was soon teaching recruits. When he was sent to officers' training school in North Carolina in 1942, she returned to Wausau, Wisconsin, to be closer to their families.

In Texas, Dad was only making $21 a month in basic training. With the current inflation rate, that is about $359 per month. His room and board were taken care of at basic camp. After my brother Merlin was born, Dad sent all of his paychecks to his wife and son. She made extra money sewing clothes and doing alterations.

Because of his college education, my dad was commissioned as a second lieutenant in anti-aircraft artillery on the last day of 1942. Before being sent overseas, he was stationed in Shelby, Mississippi, where Mom and Merlin were briefly able to visit. It would be three years before they saw each other again.

For a long time, my dad didn't talk about his experience overseas. When asked, he would say only that the war brought out the best and worst in people.

My brother Merlin recalled that Dad spoke of his war experiences "very little, hardly at all, unless we asked questions about something specific." That changed later in life after he retired from his school administrator's job.

After someone in his battalion started to organize reunions, Dad began corresponding with Army friends. I made a point to attend one of his reunions. It was revelatory to hear the things the men had experienced during the war. During conversations with these old soldiers, they chose their words carefully. At times, emotions got the best of them.

Dad became more willing to talk about what he'd experienced. In October 1999, as a Christmas present, I signed him up for an oral history interview about his involvement in the war. The Wisconsin Veterans Museum had started a program of oral histories from all the wars. All my brothers and sisters received a CD of the interview, getting to know our father better.

Around that time, my brother Merlin introduced our dad to Lowell Peterson, a cardiologist putting together a book of remembrances of World War II veterans. My father agreed to be interviewed. We were grateful. The family learned even more about Dad from that chapter.

I am extremely proud of this man, who, to my mind, epitomized that "Greatest Generation" who did their duty under the most terrifying circumstances imaginable. But he had loved his country and wanted to serve.

My dad was among the last U.S. military to leave Europe, which infuriated my mother. When he died, we found boxes with his wartime memorabilia. We discovered why he was held up in Paris and declared essential. He was going to be deployed to the Pacific Theater if President Truman decided not to bomb Japan. Dad had already served more than three years on the front lines in Italy, Germany, and France. After the atomic bomb was dropped and Japan surrendered, he made it home.

Dad told Lowell Peterson how, just before returning from overseas, he'd met a group of medics from Chicago in a town in the German Alps. "I quickly discovered that I had nothing in common with them," he said. "They had absolutely no knowledge of what our life had been like for the last three years. It seemed as though they were from another nation. I then realized that going home might be a problem. Home had not changed, but I had."

My mom and three-year-old brother Merlin were waiting for him. He said, "It was so wonderful to see them and to be home for good." But he acknowledged the adjustment. "I had lived so long in an environment of artillery shells, mortar shells, sniper fire, booby traps, and land mines that it took months to separate the war from my person."

My dad taught high school in Wausau, where I was born in August 1946. His next teaching job took our family to Brooklyn, a Wisconsin farming town south of Madison. He wanted to be a principal. Maybe he liked or had gotten used to being the captain, the head, the leader. He applied for a principal's position in Campbellsport in 1948 and got the job.

"There were five classrooms," wrote Catherine Weld in her 1954 history of Campbellsport. "In high school, there are eight teachers besides Mr. Leo Lang, the principal. About 250 students enrolled in the high school this fall." After thirty-two years of service, my father left a legacy of enrollment over 1,600 students from kindergarten through twelfth grade—bigger than the population of Campbellsport. The school bused kids in from Dotyville, seventeen miles away.

We lived in a white house on North Fond du Lac Avenue, a block from the public grade and high schools where my father worked, and where all of us kids attended high school. That was our parents' home for sixty-six years. During those years, the town grew from a couple of hundred people to two thousand today.

I lived there for eighteen years. From first through eighth grades, four of us walked to the St. Matthew's Catholic Grade

School a mile away and adjacent to the church. We walked every day, even in rain and snow. It sounds rough now, but every Catholic kid did it. There was always someone to walk with and talk with. We wore layers of clothes. During the school day, our wet pants and coats dried in the furnace room. The Catholic church in Campbellsport was the dominant church congregation, as it was in many small Wisconsin towns. Father Schwab was respected and listened to. No one questioned his authority.

In first grade, I had a bit of a lisp and took singing lessons to help it. I can remember singing in the new auditorium with Sister Hugo accompanying me on the piano. The audience was laughing. It didn't feel very good. My mother said later that I was cute and had made the people laugh. It was not comforting, as I recall, but that was the end of it.

Some of my Catholic schooldays epitomize what books and comedians make jokes about. Fifth grade was a turning point; there were sixty kids in that room, including the sixth graders. The teacher was an elderly nun, Sister Egitoria.

In those days, there was a belief that writing with the left hand was a sign of a sinner. I have never figured this out. Many years later, and asking a number of Catholics about it, no one had a clear explanation. I can only conjecture that during the crucifixion of Christ, the criminal on his right side repented. The criminal on his left side did not repent.

In fifth grade, Sister would walk up and down the aisles with a wooden ruler with a metal edge. I got hit with that ruler many times. One time, when I came home, my left hand was still bleeding. Nothing was said or done. I went to school the next day. There was never a thought of doing something different—just pull up your bootstraps!

I wasn't the only one who felt that ruler come down. But I was the only one that I can remember who developed a small stammer that year.

Many of the farm boys also got hit, often on the back of the head for falling asleep. We all knew that they had to do farm chores before they came to school. As far as I know, no one defended them from this abuse either. You did not question authority.

Some boys and girls left high school at sixteen to work on farms or in the house. Dad would try to convince their parents to keep their kids in school, at least to finish out the school year. He rarely succeeded, especially with the girls. Their parents thought the girls had enough schooling. Their mothers needed them in the kitchen. During spring planting and fall harvest, they would also help out in the fields. "What more do they need to know?" many parents asked Dad.

When I was growing up in Campbellsport, my mother hosted fabulous parties during the Christmas holidays and on other special occasions. The table settings were always precisely and beautifully set, with delicious and well-presented food. A small-town Wisconsin woman with a degree in home economics, a seamstress for her friends' daughter's wedding dresses, my mother was every bit a Martha Stewart. Her talents were never fully appreciated in our practical farming community, which may have caused frustration.

She was also an entrepreneur. For a number of years, during the Christmas holidays, she turned our family TV room into a boutique, selling beautiful handicrafts and delicious holiday food and candies. She kept the money from the sales. I think my dad understood some of her frustrations. She carefully bought beautiful furniture and china. My father would build her shelves and niches so she could see them every day.

When I was sixteen years old, a family moved in next door and forever affected my perceptions about women's rights. When the Hansen family drove up to the front curb of our house, there were three girls in their car. Their oldest was four years old. Mrs. Hansen was pregnant, due in just a few months.

When we welcomed and talked to the wife, Ann, Mom and I had a hard time catching some of her words because of her Louisiana accent. Mrs. Hansen was vibrant and talked fast. Her husband was from the Midwest like us. She had been studying biochemistry and dropped out of Tulane University to get married. The family was moving to Campbellsport so he could take over a veterinarian practice.

Time went by, and six girls later, Doc Hansen finally got his long-awaited-for son. We all sighed, thinking that his wife would at long last have some relief.

But three more girls and another boy arrived. In between those births, Mrs. Hansen was hospitalized twice with nervous breakdowns. She was treated with electronic shock therapy, which took time to recover. Both times she had to return home before being fully recovered. She had to take care of the kids.

My mother helped as much as she could. Also, being Catholic, my mother hoped there might be guidance from the church for the Hansens. There wasn't. It was such a tragedy to see what became of this giving, intelligent, and dedicated woman.

In my sophomore year, I realized I was going to have few dates because my dad was the school principal. The basketball and football players were not to drink during the season, and it was my father who enforced this rule. For the boys, underage drinking on weekends was considered a rite of passage to adulthood.

I was a cheerleader for the first three years, worked on the school newsletter, was a class officer, and was part of a girls' clique called the Crazy Eight. We were eight well-behaved, studious, and active girls in extracurricular activities. We were loyal to each other, and we trusted each other. We kept involved and had fun. After a lapse of thirty years, the Crazy Eight continued to keep in touch and meet with each other. Even though we all became very different people, we still appreciated each other.

Back then, my dad had encouraged students to help each other during study hall. That's when the farm kids needed to get most of their homework done. In the morning, many of the kids were picked up by the school bus around 7:30 a.m. after finishing morning chores. Some had to milk the cows. School started at 8:30. When they got off the bus after school, they had more chores to do. It wasn't unusual to see boys sleeping during class or study hall. Spring planting and harvest and sick animals meant longer hours of work. Needless to say, when the boys turned sixteen, most had a car to drive to school. By that age, farm kids had been driving tractors for years.

At the beginning of my junior year, the social pressure of being the principal's daughter increased. I started to stammer and stutter quite severely, in and out of school. English classes were brutal. A teacher who could be charming and thought-provoking one minute would turn into a bully the next. She had students read out loud in class, studying sentence constructions in Shakespeare's plays. When my turn came up, 90 percent of the time I couldn't say the first or second word in the sentence. I soon learned that people judge you on how you look and how you talk.

In my junior year, my teachers and my dad started to talk about college with my classmates. Even though I had been getting Bs in my classes, I was never included. At home, my parents never brought up college. I was the only one in my family who didn't go. Jane, the third child, went to a University of Wisconsin State College right after graduating from high school as did my other brother John and baby sister Marge. At the time, I didn't even question it.

Then a door opened. Our senior class took a trip to the State Capitol building in Madison. Though only eighty miles away, none of us had been to Madison. There was a lot of excitement before our trip.

After a tour of the Capitol building, we had twenty minutes of free time. Looking around me, I took in the locals—young women with flowing long hair and long skirts. The boys were playing guitars. I felt my shoulders drop. Suddenly I could breathe better and speak with ease. After I discovered bustling State Street, how could I return to Campbellsport?

Patty, one of the Crazy Eight, was talking about going to nursing school in Madison. Some of her family friends mentioned the school to her parents. Patty told me that her family was going to visit the family in Monona, right outside Madison. When I asked if I could come along, she said yes.

On that trip, I got information about St. Mary's Nursing School. I spoke to Patty and suggested we attend together and be roommates. She liked the idea, and my parents did too. They thought that if I were under the supervision of the Catholic nuns, I would be safe in that big university town.

Patty and I were thrilled when we got accepted that summer.

Three weeks before school started, Patty's mother had an aneurysm in the grocery store. It shocked the community. She had been a generous, always happy person, full of energy. She was too young for this to have happened. Patty had no choice but to stay behind and care for her three siblings and father.

I felt guilty that I was leaving while Patty's dream was cruelly thwarted. "Life wasn't fair," my father would tell me. Now I knew what he meant.

My stuttering had practically cleared up by the time I arrived in Madison. But then another upset occurred. I had two classes that semester with Mr. P. On the first day of school, he was walking up and down the aisles of desks, making jokes and being charming. He spoke about his grading system and how he set the curves. He said that there had to be a class dummy at the end of the curve. He stopped at my desk and said it was me.

We laughed, thinking it was a joke. When mid-semester tests arrived, and I received my grades, I had gotten two Fs. I talked to my classmates and learned they had more mistakes than me but had gotten better grades. Surely Mr. P. had made a mistake. I went to his office, and he reminded me about that first day of school. Being the class dummy was no joke. There was no recourse; he was the professor and I was the student. I had the same professor for another class second semester. I stayed optimistic.

I had done okay so far. But then, in the second semester another teacher had, by human error, given me a C instead of a B. She was trying to correct it in the school's new computer system. Leaving the country on vacation, she had just one day to fix it. It was ugly; the C was still in my report the next day.

After summer and working in the hospital full-time and taking clinical classes, I left the nursing school, along with twenty other girls out of a class of ninety. Their experimental curriculum was going to be revised. But it was too late for me and the others.

Returning home to Campbellsport was not an option.

I had never had a real job. In a small town like Campbellsport, I had been lucky to get babysitting jobs. Now I applied for a sales job at a locally owned department store at the minimum wage of $1.25 per hour in the women's clothing department.

I liked it and could use my sewing skills. (I had made all my clothes in high school.) I enjoyed working with people. One evening a week, I went to a sewing class at the Vocational, Adult and Technical School (Vocy Tech, now Madison College). The teacher was very kind and told me that the school had a fashion marketing two-year program. I signed up for it the next day.

This was a huge turning point in my life. After eighteen months, I had written a term paper about starting a small business and landed a job in the Executive Management Training Program at Carson Pirie Scott in downtown Chicago.

Those months at Vocy Tech were the greatest. The teachers were caring and engaging, always providing hope and encouragement. The students were focused and serious about their classes. My self-esteem and confidence soared. I was very happy and felt so fortunate. Bad experiences faded into the past, and I was going to keep them there. A wonderful and exciting year passed, and I was promoted to assistant buyer.

But I had a boyfriend in Madison who I missed. I also had my term paper on how to start a small women's clothing store. He found a store location on State Street near the University campus. I left Carson Pirie Scott in Chicago and opened a boutique called The Peacock in August 1968. The first six months were rocky. But after eighteen months, I had paid back a loan from my father, tripled my inventory, and bought a house. I had just turned twenty-four. Twenty years later, I sold The Peacock. I kept a second store, Momentum, for another six years.

I became involved in downtown city committees and volunteered to work on various projects directly with the mayors. I was paying Madison back for all it had given me.

I was appointed the commissioner for the proposed Frank Lloyd Wright Monona Terrace Community and Convention Center. As commissioner, I was recruited to a number of different roles, including community outreach for the referendum to organize a project with 11,000 inscribed tiles. After eight years working with community leaders and volunteers—all of whom loved Madison the center opened with great fanfare and success. It was my springboard into politics.

I ran for mayor of Madison in 1997 and lost in the primary to the first woman to serve as that city's mayor. At the time, it was a great personal defeat. But years later, the lessons I learned became my textbook for mentoring state and local candidates.

By the time Zach Brandon called me about an Obama fundraiser, I had morphed into a community organizer and fundraiser. Much of my success was based on people skills I had acquired while working in retail, as well as meeting the challenges of having a successful business and the gained experiences of my mother's artful parties. This combination accelerated me into Candidate Obama's National Finance Campaign Committee, his political culture, and to respect, empower, include—the antithesis of what politics was known for.

There were a few times during the Obama campaign when I asked myself why I was putting in such long hours. I already had done many volunteer projects, but this effort was turning into a day and night commitment, five to six days a week.

I wasn't building a resume or meeting a need to put "the bacon on the table." I was at the stage of my life where I could pick and choose how to spend my time, and I felt I was helping our country in my small way.

My father was an inspiration. He had done his duty in World War II, risking his life for over three years. He had been a captain fighting on the front lines in Europe, trying to do his job and keep his battalion of several hundred men alive.

There are times for all of us to stand up and be counted. As the Obama campaign progressed, I felt something more—

something not easy to articulate—that was keeping me motivated.

I would sometimes hear my father's voice in Barack's speeches or in a newspaper quote. It took a while for me to realize this. I reasoned that Obama's beloved grandfather was also a World War II veteran, and Obama would occasionally quote him. My father was in the same war at the same time. Obama's grandfather and grandmother had raised him in Hawaii while his mother was in Jakarta. By living with them from an early age, Obama had picked up the jargon of the Greatest Generation. He assimilated the quiet, confident humility of that generation of heroes. Many felt the "No drama with Obama" slogan came from the Hawaiian lifestyle, and part of it did, but the tenor of his language and his self-assurance ran deeper. I believe that is why Obama's speeches sounded so reassuring and engaging to me and many others. The connection was immediate because when he heard him speak, we subconsciously heard our fathers and grandfathers.

Would my father have voted for Obama? He was a lifelong Republican, so it wouldn't have been his usual choice. But I do recall how disturbed my dad had become when President George W. Bush did his "Mission Accomplished" publicity stunt on an aircraft carrier. At the time, the conflict in Iraq was anything but over. My father knew of President Bush's undistinguished military service record. He thought President Bush was dishonoring the uniform and what it stood for. After that incident, my father never again put out Republican candidates' signs on the front lawn.

That same year, my father granted an interview with a regional newspaper for its Memorial Day edition. He talked about how World War II had affected innocent civilians caught between the different armies marching through their towns. He told stories not found in our history books. He surprised us.

It is odd to say, but I feel there's a certain comfort that he never saw his beloved Republican Party change into what it has become today. The next generation is slowly but steadily outnumbering the Eisenhower Republican in Washington. Dad was already disturbed about the consolidation of bigger businesses, increasing ads on TV that were creating the need to consume, and less talk about the importance of education.

My father died in early November 2007. During his last months, we didn't talk about politics. That would not have made sense. Instead, we spoke of regular things: family experiences, some of his relatives who were still alive, and the weather.

Would he and my mom have voted for Barack Obama for president?

I'd like to think so. **O**

EPILOGUE:

Lessons Learned from Nine Fundraisers

"That some achieve great success is, proof to all,
that others can achieve it as well."

—Abraham Lincoln

After hosting many fundraisers with different goals and varying themes, I kept records to make my next event smoother and easier.

After each event I created a manila folder file for each of the fundraisers I had worked on—from when Barack was at the house on October 15, 2007, to "Rock for Barack" on October 25, 2008. I did this so I could easily access ideas from previous fundraisers and customize parts for different fundraisers in different cities.

I used parts of previous menus to create new menus. Also, I'd self-critique after a fundraiser and note what worked and what didn't and make suggestions for next time. I kept all the sign-in sheets from the registration table. I included printed-out emails with the sponsors of the fundraiser. This was important. They helped me recall both the donors, the volunteers, and my memory of the details.

This somewhat old-fashioned approach worked beautifully. The idea came from having my own business where I had to keep good records for tax purposes, and that process had stemmed from a class during my days at Vocy Tech. My business teacher, Mr. Wilson, had stressed the importance of good records.

I continue to use these manila folders as a resource before each fundraiser. They are organized by the host's name, the theme of the event, and the fundraiser date. There is a comfort in easily seeing and locating these files representing so many memories: organizing, calling, long days, as well as meeting and working with many wonderful people who had so much enthusiasm and optimism for our country.

When I started doing this, computers were becoming more prevalent, but they were not yet widely used for political outreach. Postal mailings were the most effective way of involving people. Now that I look back on that process, I am thankful for computers and email. They saved so much volunteer time that could be better spent getting out the vote by knocking on doors, making calls to update voters' addresses and writing postcards to seniors a few days before to remind them to vote. The email invitations saved the campaign thousands of dollars on design work, printing costs, and postage, as well as saving staff time reviewing and proofing the drafts. The email invitations also allowed the flexibility of adding new sponsor names as they confirmed their donation online or with a check. These updated invitations could be sent out numerous times.

I found that three was the magic number. But the best part about the emails was that the recipient could reply in their time with any questions.

I hope that these summaries of lessons I've learned through the last ten years might be useful to you as a template or a guide for your next fundraiser. Our most promising political candidates need our active support. As a citizen, you can help elect competent and conscientious candidates.

LESSON #1:

Be magnanimous. Invite the opposition to join your cause.

Unity Fundraiser

Thursday, July 24, 2008: 5 to 7 p.m.

Frank Lloyd Wright's Monona Terrace Community and Convention Center

Madison, Wisconsin

Hillary Clinton suspended her campaign on June 7, 2008. The superdelegate count was 246 ½ for her and 478 for Barack Obama. Ninety-nine uncommitted delegates remained.

She graciously conceded. Some days later, to allow hard feelings to subside, Clinton and Obama appeared together at a campaign rally in New Hampshire, which Clinton had won, in a hamlet called Unity. After the Unity rally, Obama appealed to his donors to help retire Clinton's debts, which had ballooned to $25 million. The response from many was "Why?" Michael O'Neil said Obama wanted to offer an olive branch and do something extraordinary to help win over Hillary's supporters.

Obama understood how long women had been waiting for their day to come. He must have thought about his grandmother

"Toot," who worked at a bank for many years. She trained a good number of young men. They would be the ones who would subsequently be offered the promotions she deserved. Toot accepted her place in the bank, even as her grandson knew she was smart and capable. There must have been signs of frustration that surfaced at home when Barry was living with them. There was a personal connection and authenticity to the idea he presented.

There was a lot of frustration with Senator Obama's win. Many Democratic women had been hoping to see a woman president this time. Madison, Wisconsin, has a progressive legacy. In the 1970s, Madison women like Representatives Midge Miller, Mary Lou Munts, and Becky Young, along with Secretary of State Vel Phillips and State Supreme Court Justice Shirley Abrahamson were in leadership roles. Since 1984, when Geraldine Ferraro was chosen by presidential candidate Senator Walter Mondale to be his running mate for vice-president, many women were hoping that a woman president would be in the near future. When Hillary was running in 2008, women were CEOs in business, and female deans and chancellors at many universities were the norm. U.S. Congresswomen Gwen Moore and U.S. Senator Tammy Baldwin were breaking through the glass ceiling in the Washington, D.C., political world. At the time, Barbara Lawton was Wisconsin's lieutenant governor. For many of their longtime supporters, having a woman president was the logical next step.

The loss for Hillary supporters was personal. She was the one who had the long list of credentials, and she was the one who had to keep proving herself for so many years. It was difficult to see a relative newcomer from the U.S. Senate win the Democratic primary election.

When Michael from campaign headquarters called a few weeks later, I was surprised to hear what he had to say. He reminded me of the unity rally in Unity, New Hampshire. He asked me to organize something similar in Madison, perhaps in a neutral public place that could hold at least 150 supporters and donors. The hope was that there would be an equal proportion of attendees from both candidates' camps. Both Barack and Hillary's donors would be asked to be sponsors. The money raised would go toward Hillary's campaign debt.

I checked in at the Monona Terrace Community and Convention Center, designed by Wisconsin's Frank Lloyd Wright. With its breathtaking views from the edge of Lake Monona, it seemed a fitting site. Monona Terrace had been controversial at the time of planning and building it. Once it was finished, though, it had a tremendously successful opening with tens of thousands of Madisonians and visitors from across the country. It has become a landmark example of getting a difficult project finished. Today it is well used and appreciated by many.

There was a charge for the facility and food and drinks. I called prominent donors from both Hillary and Obama's supporters who I expected would like this event. It was important to have those costs paid first. I started my phone calls, and in a few days, seven donors trusted me with their charge cards. I paid the facility their estimated amount for 150 guests. There was a cash bar. If some people arrived late, the food might be gone, and if more than the 150 people showed up hungry, we'd cover the cost with the donations at the doors. The "door" would be bringing in more money and would balance out the extra charge. Monona Terrace gave us a special lower rate of a nonprofit, which was gracious. Since the event was technically open to the public, they felt it was fine. I was able to bring decorations and fresh flowers for the appetizer table and small vases for the bistro tables.

Where would I get a list of Hillary's supporters to contact? The solution was to email the invitation to the fifteen to twenty friends who I knew were organizers and strong supporters of Hillary. Would they forward the invitations to their networks? I followed up with personal calls to them.

They were surprised by the idea of a unity fundraiser. Some had done unity fundraisers at the county and state primary levels, but no one could remember a unity fundraiser at this level, involving a goal for this kind of money for an opponent's campaign debt. Everyone agreed to email the invitation out at least three times. I would send them an updated sponsor list for the last two invitations. Sponsor lists showing who had already given higher amounts stimulated others to become sponsors and others to attend. In the end, we had thirty-six sponsors, an exciting show of healing and generosity, and the beginning of unity.

That night's program featured Governor Doyle, an early supporter of Senator Obama, and Dane County Executive Kathleen Falk, one of the state organizers for Senator Hillary Clinton as honorary guests. They welcomed the donors and guests and explained why they supported the unity event. Wisconsin was part of the nationwide effort.

In her speech, Kathleen emphasized, "Our primary was not only the most exciting ever; it was the most historic. Millions of people engaged, millions voted at an excitement level I have never seen in fifty-seven years. How proud and grateful I am that Senators Clinton and Obama broke barriers and changed our nation forever. As Rosa Parks said, 'We aren't where we want to be, we aren't where we are going to be, but at least, we aren't where we were.'" Kathleen continued by pointing out that her three nieces and nephews had joined her. "I want to show them my active role in doing what I can so that they aren't digging out of a bigger hole than what we have now. Wisconsin is a fifty-fifty state. In 2000, Senator Gore won by five thousand votes. Senator Kerry won by ten thousand in 2004. So I ask you to spend every possible minute over the next three months to do everything you can—writing out more checks, talking to neighbors, sending emails, driving people to the polls, to make sure we elect Senator Obama to be our next President."

Michael O'Neil came from the Chicago headquarters and did a campaign strategy presentation using David Plouffe's format and information. David was Obama's national campaign manager. The last speaker was Katherine Gehl, who was on the National Finance Committee and a former special assistant for Mayor Richard M. Daly. She talked about the importance of the country being unified in 2008. The general election would not be an easy win. Other Democratic politicians, including Senator Russ Feingold, U.S. Congresswoman Tammy Baldwin, Lieutenant Governor Barbara Lawton, and State Treasurer Dawn Marie Sass, who were listed on the invitation, supported the unity event.

Michael requested that even though this was in a public facility, "The fundraiser would be closed to the media." This was at the bottom of all the invitations. Local media respected the request.

The country would know we were all behind Candidate Obama. We would foster respect and appreciation for our candidate. After paying the cost of the room rental and food, we cleared $18,000 and played a role in helping clear Senator Clinton's debt.

LESSON #2:
Present a program tailored to your audience.

A Roasted Pig With All the Fixin's

Friday, September 5, 2008: 5 to 7 p.m.

The home of Sharon Stark and Peter Livingston

Spring Green, Wisconsin

Peter Livingston and Sharon Stark were casual friends of ours. We didn't see them that much, but when we did, the evening was invariably filled with great discussions about the news of the day, both local and national. Sharon's quick laughter at just about anything that was surprising or a bit humorous made her exceptional company. Both had successful careers with credit unions. I didn't know if they were Democrats or Independent voters. Soon after I got the first call about Senator Obama coming to my house for the fundraiser, I took a chance and phoned them.

After Sharon answered, I told her about the upcoming event with Senator Obama. She was excited and called over Peter. When I said October 15 was my planned date, Sharon groaned and said they'd be out of the country. They were disappointed to miss the event.

Both husband and wife liked Obama's positive and optimistic platform. He was different from other candidates or presidents. Even though it was used against him many times, they especially liked that he had been a community organizer.

Peter felt it would be more difficult for Hillary to win. She had become too much like a traditional politician, with overexposure and a surplus of fights on tough issues. Obama was new, refreshing in his messaging, and he didn't have her baggage.

They both loved the grassroots movement that Obama was using for his campaign. It was inclusive; everyone felt welcomed to be part of his campaign. It was full of hope and optimism. He was using a different method from any other political campaign in history, acquired as a community advocate and organizer in South Chicago.

Peter and Sharon lived in the country just a few minutes from Spring Green, the closest town to Frank Lloyd Wright's Taliesin, his original home and studio. The town was a mixture of Wisconsin farmers, artists, and retired Chicago and Madison people who wanted a lifestyle change. In the past, the couple had been involved with grassroots issues.

They liked the sincerity and genuine spirit of the people at the meetings, even though they didn't always agree with them. They organized grassroots meetings with the kind of people who demonstrated on the streets. They reminded me of the rebelling colonists during the revolutionary times of our young country. Their methods felt democratic: "We the people."

Senator Obama had a sense of what our country could be. He understood that we were always striving for a "more perfect union." He knew and said that there was no other country in the world where someone like him could succeed so well and, in such a short time, be running for president. He embodied how far the country had come.

As months passed, I spotted Sharon and Peter at several Madison fundraisers. I kept their names on my Obama email master list. After one of the fundraisers, they approached me and said they were interested in holding their own fundraiser for Obama. This was music to my ears.

Sharon was well-connected in the area and had a great list of friends. She sent out email invitations. In the past, she had overseen other fundraisers for nonprofits and had learned to be unafraid to ask for higher sponsorship amounts.

After inviting folks to the Obama event, she was surprised how supportive their friends were. Nearly everyone planned to come. The ones that didn't were out of town. Everyone offered to donate or bring their best dishes for the planned group of fifty. We expected that number from the RSVPs and Sharon's calls.

Peter had never done anything this elaborate for a political campaign. He had been prompted by an old college friend, who said Obama was important for our country, and we should do everything possible to get him elected. Both Peter and Sharon were committed to doing their best.

Peter and Sharon had to first pick two or three dates when everyone was available. They both knew a variety of people and had been living in their country home for several years. Peter thought that Jim DeVita would be a good draw. Jim was one of the principal actors and a writer at the American Players Theatre. The forty-year-old theater has a great reputation for their performances, mainly Shakespearean plays. APT has been nominated for a Tony Award for Outstanding Regional Theater.

Peter asked if Jim was a Democrat.

Yes, he was.

Was he interested? Was he in town? Two more affirmative responses followed. He was in. What would he do? Jim was going to think about it.

Peter and Sharon wanted even more headliners. I mentioned Dr. Zorba Paster. They were listeners and fans—like nearly everyone in the state—of his Saturday morning show on *Wisconsin Public Radio*. Peter and Sharon loved the idea of having Zorba.

He was incredibly popular in rural Wisconsin. His radio show had been on for over twenty years. At other events, I had seen Zorba easily engaging with people. He was an expert on Abraham Lincoln, as well as healthcare. What contrasts! But both were timely. Senator Obama was talking about an improved healthcare system in many of his speeches. Zorba had a talent for framing the politics of the day to reflect current issues. People could see and understand a different perspective of an issue and be persuasive. He used a soft and kind humor. It was brilliant. And he would also bring his book, *The Longevity Code*, for personalized signings for donors.

I knew Peter Leidy from local Saturday morning shows at our downtown cultural center, the Overture. He played the guitar and wrote lighthearted music for adults and kids. He composed many wonderful songs for the Children's Theater of Madison. I had met Peter when my daughter Muffy was in one of their productions. He was a likable and pleasant person and easy to work with. I was hoping he might donate his time and enjoy being on the same invitation with Jim DeVita and Zorba.

We managed to winnow it down to Friday, September 5 from 5 to 7 p.m. I hoped Peter would still be interested and available. When I called him, he said he was a big fan of Obama's and was more than happy to participate. He checked his calendar, and he was free that night. He wanted to know more about the event so that he could choose appropriate songs to play. I told him I would get back to him in a few days after talking with Peter and Sharon about what their other headliners would be doing at the event. They had one or two more headliners they thought might attract donors to the event.

On the day of the event, Peter had put up several signs on the curvy country roads to guide guests coming from outside the area. Even with GPS, in this hilly area, it was easy to take a wrong turn. Many of Peter and Sharon's friends from Madison drove out. Other donors came from smaller towns within a twenty-mile radius.

At the top of their driveway, on a large piece of cardboard placed on a chair, there was an agenda of each of the event's headliners, along with what they were planning to talk about and where in the home they would be. Each had fifteen minutes to speak and were encouraged to engage with the guests after they were finished with questions.

Gary Zimmer, who lived in the area, was an excellent and energizing, animated, and world-renowned speaker on new farming practices. Known as the "father of biological and organic agriculture," Gary talked about how a healthy environment would be good for better crop production.

APT actor Jim DeVita read "The Declaration of Independence." It spellbound the audience. After Jim finished, there was a solemn tone and a few questions. The seriousness of the pronouncement resonated.

Zorba repeated his talk on healthcare and how none of us could know what disease would strike our children or us. With his magic, Zorba wove that message into his talk along with Abraham Lincoln's "Gettysburg Address." Part of Zorba's magic was that he would come to a fundraiser early and listen to what the guests and hosts were talking about. He would get to know and understand his audience in a short time. He then would tailor his talk to their conversations. It was part of his success with his talks and how he managed to engage so quickly with audiences. Peter Leidy had composed a song for the event and played a repertoire of many other songs about Wisconsin—the farmers, the cheese, and our beer. It was uplifting and entertaining, making everyone smile and laugh.

Food is always important. Living out in the country, having a farm menu made sense. Food is a way to show your guests how much you appreciate them. Presentation is important. Sharon had plenty of wooden bowls and attractive platters. There was a pig roast on a spit prepared by a neighboring farmer. As the guests walked up the driveway, its aroma was tantalizing and wholesome. The event rapidly became an old fashioned barbecue with all the fixin's for dinner.

Peter and Sharon wanted as many of the ingredients as possible to come from local farms and markets. It was fall harvest time. Neighbors had been called upon to see if they would bring their most delicious family dishes like potato salads, coleslaw, oatmeal cookies, apple crisp, herbed bread and muffins. It was a real potluck. Peter and Sharon provided beverages; a local brewery donated beer, and another friend provided the wine.

We were in the country, so there was no light pollution. The weather was cooperating, and we had a warm fall evening with a starry night we could all appreciate. You could smell freshly cut hay from the neighboring fields. There were ninety-two guests; twenty-one were sponsors. Many guests stayed late.

Sharon and Peter raised nearly $19,000—more than expected. They involved so many local people with their programs and bringing food, and I expect that those folks must have then talked up or emailed the event to all their friends, driving up attendance. Or maybe the friends from Madison just wanted to be in the country for a while.

LESSON #3:
Meaningful one-on-one discussions yield results.

Fundraiser with Dr. Dennis Costakos and Anne Costakos
Friday, September 19, 2008: 6 to 8 p.m.
The Costakoses' home in the country
La Crosse, Wisconsin

I met the Costakoses through Stephen Busalacchi, the author of *White Coat Wisdom*. At the time, Steve's wife, Maureen O'Brien, was the CEO of the Wisconsin Association of Perinatal

Care—a group in which Dennis served as president. Steve asked
if members of our group could do more than our door-to-door
solicitations and check-writing. He said, "Let's get Obama's
message to more people who are undecided."

Dennis and Anne heeded the call for action. Dennis T.
Costakos has been a neonatologist for thirty years at Mayo
Clinic Alix College of Medicine and has served on its board
of directors for over eight years. He admired Senator Obama's
principles and strength through struggles.

Senator Obama had empathy for the under-represented. He
attended and received his Bachelor of Arts in Political Science
at Columbia University, then continued on to Harvard Law
School, graduating magna cum laude. Instead of taking a job
on Wall Street, Obama went to the south side of Chicago to
direct and fundraise for "Illinois Project Vote" in 1992. Later,
he became a Professor of Constitutional Law and a husband,
father, and Illinois senator. He had Midwestern grandparents
who loved him. He had Kenyan roots and spent time during
his childhood in Indonesia as well as Hawaii. Barack, with
Michelle at his side, made it clear that no matter what problem
Americans faced, whatever their differences in opinion and
experience, we were all Americans. New, old, urban, rural,
suburban—we can find common ground.

Dennis concluded that Senator Barack Obama was not
alone in his quest. This young candidate for president had
an extraordinarily accomplished and charismatic wife named
Michelle Obama. She grew up on the south side of Chicago,
attended Princeton and then Harvard Law School. When she
met Barack, he was a former community organizer, who saw

the great potential of true democracy. They did their work with respect and class. Dennis and Anne Costakos thought America could use another Jackie Kennedy Onassis. The United States needed them, as did the world.

Dennis and Anne had also read President Obama's book, *The Audacity of Hope*. He told me, "We both agreed and were convinced that his focus on education and healthcare would be important and good for the country.

"Both Barack and Michelle Obama showed that they could embrace popular culture as well as high culture. They would do this in the most ethical style during the campaign while still parenting Malia and Sasha. They both kept their authenticity and kept consistent their messages of hope and opportunity for all and change for a better and more inclusive country." Indeed, wise words from Dennis.

There was less than a week left to prepare for the fundraiser at their partially vacated home on eleven acres of land, set in a valley of almost four hundred acres. It was in a rural setting but only a few minutes' drive from La Crosse. With GPS, we hoped people would be able to find it.

Much of the food was homemade, though some was catered from Festival Foods. There was delicious barbeque from Famous Dave's. Sam's Club had the best shrimp. Panera's bread and pastries were offered as well. When I arrived at six o'clock, I saw Congressman Ron Kind was already there, throwing a football with his children. Later, in the main room, Dr. Zorba was a big draw, and anyone that did not know him nevertheless enjoyed and appreciated his talk. Zorba inspired us all by reciting the Gettysburg Address, stressing the importance of the union. All the guests were engaged and asked him many questions afterward. He autographed his book of *The Longevity Code*. Stephen Busalacchi autographed his book *White Coat Wisdom*.

More than a hundred people of all ages and walks of life came. Some were in the house, while others were outside on the tennis court, where games were set up. There were farmers there, some of whom I knew had never voted for a Democrat. There were also teachers, short-order cooks, musicians, and homemakers. Many doctors, midwives, nurses, and University students showed up, as healthcare was an important issue for them. Anne and Dennis knew only about 50 percent of the people there. We did end up making lifelong friends that day. But just as importantly, at that point, many of the people who came were undecided in their vote. We were happily overwhelmed.

Deep and thoughtful discussions continued as the evening progressed. Opinions were offered on the need to keep more Americans healthy through both personal and societal responsibility. One of the attendees was the CEO of Sentry Foods, who was married to a professor. He was persuaded that good business was not possible unless healthcare became a national priority. Other people better understood that education cannot improve unless education becomes a national priority. Both of these were talking points in Obama's vision for a better America. Dennis said, "The bottom line was we made the point to the guests that night: this Barack fellow was not being shortsighted in his vision of America. He believed in our America. He believed in democracy."

Dennis spoke to a CEO of a $500 million food chain who lived in La Crosse. His wife was a professor at the University of Wisconsin–La Crosse. He had received an email invitation, most likely from a friend of a friend. He was on the fence about whom he intended to vote for and had a number of questions about Obama.

Dennis listened, and they volleyed back and forth. In the end, he realized that good health was important for his employees. He would vote for Obama. The socializing and discussions continued until almost 11 p.m. when the clean-up started. The event was well worth it.

LESSON #4:

Democracy is for the young and the old.

Family Fall Festival

Friday, September 26, 2008: 5 to 8 p.m.

Doc's home/Kathy and Ellen

Madison, Wisconsin

Kathy told me that during a casual conversation while driving her young son Josh and his friend Jason to a soccer practice had made her think of doing a fundraiser for Obama. She was telling them about a fundraiser that she had helped with the day before. It was about same-sex marriage, which wasn't yet a law in Wisconsin. Support was building, and events around this issue were popular. Josh said that his family with two moms was just as nice as Jason's family who had a mom and a dad.

Jason asked where all the raised money went. Kathy said it was "to help make all kinds of families okay." They both agreed it was fine to have two moms, two dads, a mom and dad, or a mom or a dad. The conversation shifted to who was going to be the next president.

The kids wanted to have a president who thought like they did—that all kinds of families were okay. These innocent words of acceptance inspired Kathy and her partner Ellen to do a fundraiser for Senator Obama, who was raised by a single mom and her parents. Other issues concerned Kathy's family, including a country in distress, the Iraq War, the collapsing housing market, and the unstable stock market.

Kathy and Ellen were both well-connected medical doctors. They lived in a friendly and liberal area of Madison and knew many of their neighbors. Their spacious home would be ideal for a fundraiser.

One of their friends, another physician named Melissa, had been to Obama fundraisers at my home. Melissa called me and asked if I could help out Kathy and Ellen since this would be their first fundraising event.

It was, of course, my pleasure.

At home, Kathy and Ellen made their own welcoming 8 x10 invite, with the header Family Fall Festival Fundraiser and an Obama "Hope" sign.

They wanted special guests in attendance who would attract more donors and asked if I would contact a popular politician. They suggested Mayor Dave Cieslewicz, Congresswoman Tammy Baldwin, State Representative Mark Pocan, and Senator Russ Feingold.

Michael O'Neil from the Obama campaign arranged for an internet link so donors signing up for the event could easily pay online. He would let us know who was signing up and at what amounts. Their names would be included in the next distribution. We planned three email distributions.

Kathy and Ellen wanted their guests to be able to give however much money they wanted. In most conversations, I suggested $250. Kathy, Ellen, and Melissa were surprised at how easy it was to talk to people about the fundraiser and ask for money. After discussing sponsorship, folks checked their calendars and returned their calls.

I sent the electronic invitation to my Obama list. Melissa had sent the electronic invitation to colleagues and friends who might be interested. A few days later, I made calls for $250 per person to the people I knew who were in the medical world in Madison and to others who had young kids.

The day came, and the weather was good—another brilliant fall day. When I arrived, on their lawn was a giant inflatable bouncing castle with a big homemade sign by the kids that said "Bouncing for Barack."

What a great idea. Kathy had thought of it, though her son, Josh, must have had something to do with the idea. It was a big success. Every kid who arrived gravitated to it. Their parents looked relieved when they saw it. Many kids spent nearly all their time bouncing and went home tired.

For this event, no one needed to worry about getting a babysitter. That helped persuade people to join us.

Many neighbors brought their most delicious dishes. There was a plentiful and healthy potluck buffet on the dining room table.

The evening went fast. Ellen oversaw a small program. She thanked the donors and everyone who joined us. Mayor Dave gave a brief talk about getting all of our friends out to vote for this historic presidential election. Senator Feingold and Executive Falk arrived after the program and mingled with the guests. We were happy that they all could join us and that the guests could meet them.

There were about eighty-five to one hundred adults and kids at the event. It was a good night, and everyone was happy. They raised $11,252.

LESSON #5:

Enlist locals. Avoid being seen as an outside agitator.

A Grand Affair

Friday, October 3, 2008: 5:30 to 7:30 p.m.

Jan Viste's home

Oshkosh, Wisconsin

With a population of about 65,000, Oshkosh sits on Lake Winnebago, one of the biggest inland lakes in the United States. It is also home to the Experimental Aircraft Association (EAA), an international organization of aviation enthusiasts. Every summer, that event features over 10,000 planes and attracts over 500,000 visitors (EAA, 2019). The University of Wisconsin–Oshkosh has 10,294 students (University of Wisconsin–Oshkosh, 2018–19). It is a "purple" voting city: sometimes blue for Dems, other times red for Republicans.

When Steve Busalacchi called and connected me to Dr. Costakos, he also mentioned Jan Viste, the widow of a well-respected doctor who had served Oshkosh residents for many years. Steve phoned her about having a fundraiser for Senator

Obama, and Jan liked the idea. He gave me her phone number and email address. I called her the next day.

She was very interested in Candidate Obama and wanted to support him as much as she could. I assured Jan that having a fundraiser at her home would make a difference for the campaign. Thinking about the event, she said she knew and supported their first-term State Assemblyman Gordon Hintz and wanted him as a guest. He was running for a second term. Since her former husband was a doctor and, knowing Steve, I asked her if she might also like to have Dr. Zorba Paster from *Wisconsin Public Radio* as a speaker.

Like everyone else, Jan was a fan of Zorba's weekly Saturday morning shows. She had friends who were also devoted to his Saturday morning radio show, and they'd be thrilled to meet him.

I told her that I'd call him right after our phone call and see when he was available. Chances of Zorba attending would increase if we worked around his schedule. I asked Jan for some dates that would work for her. I could only hope one of them would coordinate with Zorba's calendar.

She offered that she had a good list of people who would be interested, and she would contact them. That was a relief and very important since at the time, my Obama list had only names from the greater Madison area. Jan Viste sounded familiar with the process of giving dinner parties and receptions. Later, I learned that she had been active with community nonprofits and had done numerous benefits for them. I asked if she could cover the cost of appetizers, wine, and sodas. She said that she had a caterer and would cover the costs. I thanked her profusely.

I called Steve to save Jan's dates. Then I called Zorba and left a message to return my call. He did call back, and we found a date and time that would work. I again asked him if he would bring copies of his book *The Longevity Code* and sign them for donors.

We arranged to ride together to Jan's house on Lake Winnebago. The next day I got back to Jan to confirm the date and time. She was thrilled and would call Gordon, hoping he was also available. She would also contact her caterer. Jan had at least thirty to forty donors attending. Some were re-arranging their calendar to make it. I called Steve about the time and asked him to bring forty books. I called Roz, Michael's assistant from the campaign, and asked if she would design an online invitation with a donation link. I emailed her the necessary information: who, what, when, and where. The invitation would include Jan's list, Steve's shorter list of friends and colleagues, and my three personal contacts. Roz emailed it the next day, and I forwarded it to Jan and Steve.

After the invitation arrived, I asked Roz if the campaign had any previous donors in the Oshkosh area and surrounding towns. If so, could she send me their names and phone numbers?

That day, twenty-four pages arrived on my computer. I first picked out the Oshkosh names to call about the event. My calls to those on the list took extra time because many of the people answering the phone didn't know Jan or me and had to think about it. It was a reminder that people wanted to know more about the person organizing the event.

They weren't as trusting when speaking to a stranger from Madison. Finally, I noticed and stopped saying that I was from Madison. That helped. Back in the 1960s, Madison was one of the national centers of student unrest and weekly protests against the war in Vietnam. The capital city still hadn't shaken its perceived notoriety throughout the state. Also, the suggested donation was $100, which was somewhat high for that area.

I ran out of time before calling the names on the next tier of donors—those for whom I had to track down their towns on a map and determine if they were close enough to make the drive to Oshkosh.

A few days later, I checked in with Jan to see if she had any questions or needed any help. She was optimistic and still contacting a few more friends on her list. Some wanted to bring a friend. I checked with Roz the next day. Donations were coming in online from the link on the invitation.

On Friday morning, Steve called. He was frustrated, but things had not worked out and he could not come. However, he delivered forty-two signed copies of his book to my home. He had already phoned Jan and asked how many guests would be coming. Jan thought forty or fifty and mentioned that the couples most likely would take one book.

That afternoon, Zorba and I drove up to Oshkosh to Jan Viste's home, a beautiful brick, cable-roofed historic home on a large lot with an extended shoreline overlooking Lake Winnebago. It was both stately and inviting. When we entered, it was amazing to see how wonderfully Jan had everything organized. A neighbor would staff the registration table. The dining table looked like Martha Stewart had orchestrated it.

Every detail had been thought out. The dining room opened onto a large, attractive, and comfortable living room. Yes, this house had seen many receptions and dinners.

Zorba got his books organized at a table in the living room for signing after the program. Steve's books were on the table too, already inscribed.

Representative Gordon Hintz arrived early. He, Zorba, and I discussed what he wanted to do for the program. Out of respect and because he knew the local audience better than us, Gordon made the decisions for the program. Usually, politicians are flexible and ready to speak; it's part of their job. Even though this was Gordon's first term, he was confident and made good suggestions.

People began arriving. Within about forty-five minutes, the living and dining rooms had about fifty guests. In the living room, Gordon welcomed them and thanked Jan for her hospitality. He made remarks about one or two issues that were being discussed at the Capitol and the work ahead for getting out the vote.

He introduced Zorba. As usual, Zorba had been mixing with the guests and familiarizing himself with them as he listened to conversations. He had customized his talk, speaking about the importance of the Affordable Care Act (ACA) but not using its widespread nickname of Obamacare. He had sensed undecided voters in the room. He took questions, which the guests appreciated.

Gordon closed the program and directed guests to Zorba's table to pick up their personalized signed copy of his book. The guests were excited about receiving both signed books. Some were taken as presents for friends or family members unable to attend.

By seven o'clock most of the guests had left. All of Steve's books were gone. Zorba had brought extra books and distributed most of them.

We thanked Jan for opening up her splendid home, for organizing the event and covering costs, and for her work making the calls. It all made the fundraiser successful. I collected the checks and credit card forms and would Fed Ex them to Roz.

Roz soon called back. There was a glitch in the donor link on the invitation. That was the first and only time there was a problem. But she was flexible and hardworking. Roz hand-sorted the data and felt confident that we had brought in nearly $5,000. I passed on the good news to Jan, Gordon, Steve, and Zorba and thanked them again for the success.

LESSON #6:
Engage voters on the issues.
Focus on the Issues
Sunday, October 12, 2008: 1 to 3 p.m.
Imperial Garden Restaurant
Carol Koby and Denis Carey
Middleton, Wisconsin

At Sharon Stark and Peter Livingston's Spring Green fundraiser for Obama, I was surprised to see someone whom I had not seen for quite some time. There was Carol Koby, whom I believed to be a Republican, standing with her husband in a field of prairie grass amidst all these Democrats at a fundraiser for Senator Obama. How could it be?

Carol and I had known each other for years. We had mutual friends, and our paths often crossed at community events. I knew she was a former "Alice in Dairyland," an "only-in-Wisconsin" state employee hired each year to promote Wisconsin's dairy and agricultural industry. Carol had also worked for Republican Governor Knowles in the Wisconsin Capitol in the 1960s.

When I saw her that day in the countryside outside Spring Green, I immediately went over and said, "What are you doing here? I thought you were a Republican."

"Not anymore," she said.

My first thought was that if Senator Obama's candidacy could convince Carol to become a supporter, maybe we had a good chance of winning. She filled in the blanks, sharing with me the reasons that brought her to this political place.

Carol's background was in media communications, a result of her on-the-job experience as Alice. After a year on that unique job, she finished her last two years of college at the University of Wisconsin–Madison, majoring in Communication Arts with a focus on radio and television broadcasting. A few years later, she became the first woman director at WITI-TV6 in Milwaukee. Because of family needs, she returned to Madison where her career broadened over the next decades to include director of consumer affairs at WKOW-TV, marketing consultant for a national women's health organization, and moderator of *Picture of Health*, a cable television program produced by the University of Wisconsin Hospital and Clinics.

Carol added to her education credentials by returning to UW–Madison on her fiftieth birthday to obtain a master's degree in Continuing and Vocational Education with a focus on women and health. In early 2002, Carol was asked by Mid-West Family Broadcasting to develop a radio program to discuss issues important to an aging population. That spring, she developed and launched the new program, *All About Living*, and is still producing and hosting this popular weekly program eighteen years later.

In Spring Green, Carol said it was the totality of her life experiences—professional and personal—that brought her to the realization of how critical it was for everyone to have access to healthcare, a topic often explored by the professionals she interviewed on her broadcasts. That led her to become an advocate for affordable, accessible healthcare. It was why she was at a backyard fundraiser for Barack Obama.

While she saw access to affordable healthcare as the most important issue, there were other reasons why she abandoned her Republican leanings. She had been watching CNN late on March 9, 2003, and was dismayed to see bombs dropping on the city of Baghdad. The George W. Bush administration had preemptively ordered the attack based on the supposed belief Iraq had weapons of mass destruction. That belief turned out not to be true. Carol was sickened by what she saw and the spin that followed from the Bush administration.

Then there was an American economy and a recession that had left so many people financially underwater. The Bush administration had gotten us to this point. Something needed to be done! Something needed to change!

Carol concluded by saying, "It does not matter if Barack Obama is male or female, black or white. He is obviously bright, impressive, a great communicator, and he is saying the right things—things I want to hear. He is proposing to fix the economy and make affordable healthcare available to the millions of Americans who were locked out of the system." He is also opposed to the Iraq War and the actions of the Bush administration."

Carol asked what I was doing. I told her about the fundraisers I had organized for Senator Obama.

She and her husband Denis looked at each other. Carol told me they'd like to do a fundraiser. Just like that! Neither one had ever before staged a fundraiser, but both were avid Obama enthusiasts. When I told them I'd support their effort and be available to help, they decided on the spot to do it.

From one fundraiser to the next!

Over the next couple of days, Carol and I volleyed ideas back and forth about what shape the fundraiser should take. Carol wanted to have a "conversation" in which voters could learn more about the issues. That was something new, and I thought it could get the attention of undecided voters—possibly attracting Independents.

Many of Carol's friends and acquaintances were Independent or moderate Republicans. Her list could be a whole new audience. Would they be curious and open enough to come and make a $50 donation? I didn't know.

I would also distribute the invitation to my Obama list of nearly six hundred active donors, mostly in the greater Madison area. Now we needed to build a strong lineup of speakers on relevant issues to attract people. This was a fundraiser, not a meet and greet or reception.

Carol and I were getting excited about the potential of reaching a new pool of potential Obama voters. The November 4 presidential election was just six weeks away. The entire nation—and much of the world—was talking about who would win. The polls were coming in every few days with varying margins.

But where would the fundraiser be held? Carol and Denis's condo was too small to hold a large group of people.

During this planning and organizing period, Carol and Denis went out for dinner one night at Imperial Garden, a neighborhood Chinese restaurant. The Middleton restaurant was well established, popular, and quite large.

During dinner, the owner, Karen Meyer, an acquaintance, came over to say hello.

Carol and Denis mentioned their idea for a fundraiser and asked if she ever made Imperial Garden available for such an event. She said yes, and when they told her it would be for Barack Obama, she didn't hesitate to say she'd work with them on it.

The next day, Carol asked me to check out the restaurant. Imperial Garden was in Middleton, also known as "The Good Neighbor City." The restaurant was well located on a busy corner, with plenty of available parking. It had many large rooms, plenty of areas for people to register, mingle, and gather for the planned program. The restaurant didn't open until 4 p.m. on Sundays, so we selected a Sunday that worked well with the campaign and did not interfere with the Green Bay Packers football game. (Ironclad Wisconsin rule: Schedule around Packers games.) We began planning for a 1 to 3 p.m. event on October 12.

We had four weeks to plan and organize. Carol created the theme "Focus on the Issues: A Fundraiser for Barack Obama." We chose to profile what Carol considered the two top issues: the economy and healthcare. Because of her media experience, Carol had many connections in the community. She researched and developed a list of well-respected speakers who could speak about those two crucial issues and how policy decisions impacted them.

A "Save the Date" was emailed to our combined list, stating that Senator Herb Kohl and other speakers would attend as well. Two more invitations were sent later with a more complete list of speakers and guests.

The suggested donation at the door would be $50. Carol wanted to make sure the amount was acceptable for those who could not afford more, or anyone who might be on the fence but wanted to hear more about the issues and how they applied to Candidate Obama. While such a voter may not want to contribute a lot, they still might vote for Obama if they heard the right reasons to do so.

We discussed what the sponsorship levels should be. Carol heard from some potential sponsors that they had contributed several times to the Obama campaign. They were hesitant to make another large contribution but still wanted to be a part of the event. To use their name on the email invitation, which would attract more attendees, Carol decided to give them credit for what they had already given and suggested they only needed to contribute to be part of the event.

The last emailed invite had an impressive group of speakers. Wisconsin Governor Jim Doyle served as honorary host, and the program now included both of our U.S. Senators Herb Kohl and Russ Feingold. The guest panelists were Don Nichols, University of Wisconsin Professor Emeritus of Economics and Public Policy, who spoke on "Bailouts vs. Recessions." Melanie Ramey, Wisconsin state president for the League of Women Voters and Dr. Jonathan Jaffery, chief medical officer of the Wisconsin Medicaid Program, spoke on healthcare reform.

Dr. Zorba generously made another appearance, signing his book, and Steve Busalacchi offered his wisdom, along with signed copies of his book.

The day of the event, Carol, Denis, and I arrived before noon. When we entered Imperial Garden's main dining room, we saw that the staff had reconfigured the room into a theater-style setup, with a draped table at the front. It looked great. We were hoping to seat 150, and there were nearly 200 chairs. That scared us a bit because we wanted the room to look and feel full and not have a lot of empty chairs. We needed people to show up!

The bar and refreshments were in another room. Karen had offered to have an open cash bar and provide appetizers at cost. Considering the bountiful table of appetizers she provided and the nominal fee she charged us, we were fairly sure it turned out to be below cost for us.

Through Carol's media connections, she was able to obtain a professional sound system, so all our speakers would be clearly heard. Denis set it up and tested it.

We set up the registration table in a large entranceway. We asked everyone to sign in and give their phone number and email address. This information is invaluable. It would be given to Michael and entered into the Obama campaign's database for updates and requests for more donations during the final weeks of the campaign. Three volunteers arrived to get their instructions about working the registration table, how to record checks and credit card numbers, and, of course, have the guests sign in. Dr. Zorba Paster and Steve Busalacchi were positioned with their books between the registration table and the second, smaller room off the entrance where there were delicious Chinese appetizers and the cash bar.

The senators and speakers arrived around 12:40 p.m. We ushered them up to the head table and asked them to test their microphones. They were surprised to see how many chairs were set up, and some went right to their notes for a quick review.

We were ready to go before one o'clock. Carol, Denis, and Karen said that from the comments they were getting, they sensed a lot of enthusiasm for the event. I was hoping they were right.

People had already started to arrive. Then a long line formed in the entrance area and out the front door. Carol directed the guests into the large room. I helped at the registration table to keep the line moving. People were patient. They, too, were surprised to see the long line.

Adrenaline was kicking in for Carol and me. By one o'clock, the room was nearly full, and people were still arriving. It was soon standing room only.

Carol welcomed everyone and reminded them about the signed books given to donors by Dr. Zorba and Steve Busalacchi, the cash bar, and appetizers—all of which would be available again following the program. Carol introduced Governor Jim Doyle, who opened the program.

Wisconsin Senior Senator Herb Kohl was next, followed by Senator Russ Feingold. They spoke of the political landscape in Wisconsin and cited the importance of the type of leadership and opportunities we would get in an Obama administration. They shared personal insights into working with Senator Obama as a Senate colleague. They talked about the weakening economy due to housing failures. Senator Kohl reminded the audience of his leadership addressing the broad needs of a growing aging population. Senator Feingold underscored his commitment to the economic health of our historically strong dairy and agriculture industries.

Professor Don Nichols gave examples of the current fickle economy. On September 15, Lehman Brothers had filed the largest bankruptcy action ever. The housing market was unstable. Professor Nichols explained how policies made in Congress affect everyday people. What do regulation and non-regulation mean to the average citizen? The professor encouraged attendees to study the issues and listen to the candidates, to understand the policies they were proposing, and what they were promising.

Melanie Ramey, the Wisconsin president of the League of Women Voters, explained how the structure of Medicare and Medicaid could provide guidance for creating a similar system for everyone in this country. She pointed out how some people criticize Medicare because it is a government program. She explained that it is an excellent example of a public-private partnership. The government collects the premium and makes the rules, but private insurance companies pay the claims.

As an example, she described that the main business of a large, local insurance company oversaw and implemented Medicare and Champus, the military health program.

Melanie also commented that people get hysterical about socialized medicine, saying, "We don't want that here!" She said the U.S. actually has one of the purest examples of socialized medicine in the world: the Veterans Affairs system. Basically, in the VA system, the government hires doctors and staff, and the government pays them.

It was a full program at Imperial Garden. All the speakers were engaging, knowledgeable, and energized by the large audience, and the attendees listened intently. We had two microphones available for the audience, and well thought out and courteous questions were taken after each speaker. At the end, Carol thanked the speakers and the audience for coming and for their support of Barack Obama for president. She reminded them to vote and to get to know each other before they leave, enjoy the refreshments, and not to forget their signed books.

We ushered everyone into the next room as graciously as possible. It was just approaching 3:30 p.m. The restaurant staff began the task of returning the room to its original state to open for business at four o'clock.

As we began packing everything up, we noted that both authors had run out of their books.

They thought that one hundred books each would have been plenty.

This fundraiser was considered one of the most successful among those that purposely attracted smaller donors who were exploring the issues and desiring to learn more. Our final tally showed we had fourteen "hosts," who each donated $500. Twenty-three "supporters" donated $250 each. Most attendees paid $50, and suggesting a donation of $50 allowed eight people to pay less and join us and still feel welcome. We were happy to have raised $16,680 for Senator Obama that Sunday afternoon. We all went home exhausted but delighted with the results.

The next day, Carol and I wrote our thank you notes to Karen and the Imperial Garden staff. We continued to hear positive comments about the event in the weeks that followed.

The format of structuring events that focus on educating and bringing in the Independent voters is one that I continue to use today. People want to be engaged. They are interested in hearing the facts behind the current issues and how they fit with the candidates' positions.

In crafting our democracy/republic, our founders based its success on having an informed electorate. I remain committed to that pursuit.

LESSON #7:

If possible, use star power.

Bradley Whitford Event

Sunday, October 19, 2008: 4 to 6 p.m.

Sollinger home

Madison, Wisconsin

We had an extraordinary experience with Bradley Whitford, who played Josh Lyman, the White House deputy chief of staff in the popular and long-running TV series, *The West Wing*.

I got a call from Michael O'Neil on a Tuesday afternoon. Michael said that he was trying to arrange an Obama fundraiser with Bradley for this coming Friday, just four days away. He had to work around Bradley's busy schedule but was eager to promote the candidate by using Bradley's considerable star power.

He was also a local; Bradley grew up in Madison. On Wednesday afternoon, Michael confirmed that Bradley would be arriving in Madison Sunday afternoon. I told him that I would be gone on Saturday and Sunday and that Heidi Wilde would be in charge of the proposed event, even if it was held at my house.

She and I had become friends during the year, and Heidi volunteered for a number of fundraisers. Michael hesitated for a second, then said, "That's fine, Mary. I can trust you." Michael said that he was working on the invitation with the donation internet link. He would try to get all that information to me in the morning.

It was at the end of the campaign, with only two and a half weeks until November 4. I knew that Michael was under an enormous amount of pressure from some of the other swing states and expected that he might be late in getting the invitation to me.

That night I decided to email my Obama list for the Madison area:

Hello, all. Please excuse this group email, but there is a time issue. Today I found out that the actor Bradley Whitford is coming THIS Sunday from 4–6 p.m. to our home for a fundraiser. There is not time to contact others for the use of their home as a location. Because I have a family commitment, I will be leaving town Saturday morning. My husband, Hans, will be your host with the support of some great and dedicated Obama supporters and volunteers.

Two things: First, would you like to be a sponsor? $1,000 for host couple, $400 per couple, and $150 per guest.

Second, would you be willing to make calls to your friends who enjoy *The West Wing* and see if they would like to be a sponsor?

Headquarters will be sending an invitation with an internet link for your donation tomorrow, and I will forward it to you as soon as I receive it.

Here are some talking points in case people need convincing:

1. Even though Wisconsin is ahead today in double digits, we don't know what will happen in the next sixteen days. One day can end a political win. Remember, Jimmy Carter led polls by double digits about Reagan at this point in that election.

2. We have to win BIG in Wisconsin so that Republicans and/or Attorney General Van Hollen won't debate or contest a close win. Kerry won by .4 percent and Gore by .2 percent—both less than a single percentage point.

3. This event will be for the Committee for Change. All funds raised will go only to the battleground states, including Wisconsin. We must win Ohio, Florida, and/or Colorado. These states are traditionally Republican.

4. Most likely, this will be the last event with a surrogate.

FYI: Bradley Whitford of *The West Wing* was born in Madison and attended Madison East High School.

Many thanks to you all for your valuable time and energy.

Yes, We Can!

Mary LS

The next day, I had a plan ready to go. First, I called the volunteer foodies from the October 15 Obama fundraiser. All agreed to help. Heidi, Melissa, and Marilyn could come early on Sunday morning and make the food.

I made out the menu and grocery list. At my computer, I saw the invitation had arrived. Michael had been right on time. My list had grown to over four hundred donors. I knew Bradley would draw a good crowd. Since the event had been organized on such short notice, there would be a smaller crowd. I planned for fifty to sixty.

I took my planned menu and went to the grocery store and bought the food. On Friday afternoon, Heidi and Melissa came over, and we went through the details. We set up the living room for the event. We moved tables and chairs around and set up the registration table in the front entry. Two UW students, Jennifer and Sam, had volunteered to work the guest registration table.

Twenty-four hours after the invitation was emailed out, thirty-five people had donated. This was a great indication that the fundraiser would be a success, in spite of the small window for organizing and guests clearing their calendars. I called in the wine order to our neighborhood liquor store, and they were happy to make the delivery on Sunday.

Saturday, I left on a morning flight, feeling good. I got only one call on Sunday morning from Heidi—no big problem.

Hans phoned after the event and said it had been a great success. There were over eighty donors and just enough food. Melissa had to run next door for more plates. My neighbor Ann had left plates on her kitchen table in case we needed them. Bradley had spoken to the crowd about the importance of a Wisconsin win for Barack. He was personable and walked around the room, meeting guests. He was fun too. Bradley poked fun at Hans. Bradley said to him, "In the many years I have been in Hollywood and making movies, you have the fakest German accent I've ever heard."

Everyone, including Hans, broke into roaring laughter. Hans arrived in Madison when he was twenty-nine, and to this day he has a strong accent. Long after the event, he was still being teased about his "fake" German accent.

More great memories for many people. The campaign was happy too; the fundraiser brought in $28,175.

LESSON #8:

Trust your gut.

Rock for Barack

Saturday, October 25, 2008: 7:30 p.m.

Peggy Hedberg's historic home

Madison, Wisconsin

Roberta was a friend who had supported Hillary until June, when she conceded to Obama. I had called her for the July Unity Fundraiser, asking if she and her husband, Lester, would be sponsors. When she said yes, I thought it was a good sign for Hillary Democrats coming over to support Obama. Roberta and Lester were high profile Dems in Madison. Their public support for Obama would influence others who may still be on the fence about Hillary.

Roberta called me in mid-October. She was very excited about doing an event at the end of the month. This would be the last fundraiser of the campaign cycle.

I was hesitant. Madison had had seven major fundraisers in the past eight months. People had been very generous. Would yet another fundraiser be well received? I asked Roberta why she was so excited.

She was hearing more and more enthusiasm for Senator Obama. Some of this was coming from Independents. In addition, Carol's fundraiser at Imperial Garden on October 12 had left certain conservatives re-thinking who they would be voting for. It all made sense. Why not just do it? Roberta also had mutual friends who wanted to help out.

We divided up the tasks right away. She would contact Governor Doyle and the first lady to be special hosts. Roberta was serving in the governor's cabinet at the time, so she had a clear and fast connection. Also, Roberta would contact legendary musicians Ben Sidran, Gerri DiMaggio, and Leotha Stanley. She would design an electronic invitation. She would take care of receiving the donations.

Roz from Obama headquarters emailed forms for check and credit card donations. It would be emailed with the invitations. The deadline was two days before the event. The invitation stressed that space would be limited. Mary needed to find a large house that would be accessible, organize the foodie volunteers, buy the food for six desserts, and bring flowers for the dining room table and bar area. I wanted to use china plates and nice wine glasses. We planned to make it a high-dollar event with a five-star atmosphere.

At the end of the next day, Roberta and I connected. Roz had already emailed us the campaign form for the donations. The governor and all the musicians were committed for Saturday, October 25.

Peggy Hedberg, who had hosted the first 2008 Obama fundraiser in February, was happy to again open her stunning historic home for the last fundraiser. She also agreed to cover the wine and beverage costs. We could use her china dessert plates and wine glasses, along with mine. Wendy Skinner would contact her friend who was a licensed bartender. The foodie volunteers from the October 2007 fundraiser were also excited about working at the last fundraiser before the election. It would be easier this time; we were just doing desserts. The volunteers would arrive at 2 p.m. on the day of the fundraiser and start baking. As usual, they would also stay and help clean up.

Peggy also had a friend who made calls to the neighbors. Some neighbors were not able to afford the donation, or their spouses were still undecided and didn't want to make a large donation. But they still wanted to participate. They were asked to bring their best desserts. It was an opportunity to practice respect, empower, include. I had contacted two local businesses who were Dems and asked for donated dessert plates for fifty people. Coming to our aid was Madison's best European cheese store, Fromagination. Also donating delicious food was the popular restaurant, Marigold Kitchen, which had a farm-to-table concept. We were hoping for 150 donors.

I again promised Peggy that her home would be left in perfect shape. She had guests arriving the following day.

Roberta, Peggy, and I were so excited. Everything was falling into place. I remember sending out a regular email to my Obama list with the details and the donation form. The sponsor levels were $500 per person for Gold Hosts and $250 per person for Silver Hosts. At the door, it was $100 per person. We were receiving many calls and replies from the emailed invitations.

The next morning, October 20, Roberta had designed an attractive and colorful 8 x 10 invitation headlined "Rock for Barack Concert." With the form, we sent out the invitation to our lists, then to Peggy and Wendy for their lists. Wendy made calls. People only had a three-day window to reply.

On Friday afternoon we sent out the invitations with nearly a hundred sponsors that were paid or pledged. Roberta was overwhelmed with donations in the mail and pledges through email.

On Saturday, the foodie volunteers, Michelle, Heidi, and Mimi, arrived at 2 p.m. I brought my wine glasses and china plates with anticipation that we would have a full house. Because of the strong response, we increased the quantities for most of the recipes just to make sure that there were plenty of desserts. Guests could always take them home. The plates from the two businesses had arrived and were beautifully arranged. The musicians arrived by five o'clock to set up and tune their sound systems. Roberta brought her donor list of pledged and paid contributions for the registration table. Friends of Wendy's were volunteering at the registration table at the front door.

We opened the doors early when we saw guests coming up the long front sidewalk. It was about 7:15 p.m. There was a small but continuous line. The house was filling up, the music was playing, and people were sipping their wine and eating. Within a half an hour, the living room was filled and overflowing into the winter porch.

The governor and first lady arrived around 8 p.m. The room was teeming with excitement and intense conversations over the idea that Obama could actually win. He had done well in the October debates against Senator McCain. The polls were promising.

By 8:30, all the wine glasses were in use, and we moved onto Peggy's glass juice glasses—a good problem. Roberta started the program by welcoming the guests, thanking hostess Peggy and all the sponsors. She introduced the governor, and he spoke about the importance of voting. She told us to remind all our friends and relatives and colleagues to get out to vote. She wanted Wisconsin to turn blue for Senator Obama. We would be making history. Roberta ended the program with an "ask" to consider making another donation for Obama.

Some did. The music started to play again, and Gerri DiMaggio sang a few more songs. After talking with more guests, the governor and first lady left. By nine o'clock, people started to leave with a spring in their step. They had energized each other with their conversations and enthusiasm.

The foodie volunteers did double duty, washing and recycling plates and glasses and checking out the first floor of the house. We went through the house a couple of times just to make sure that everything was in the same shape as before the event. We had plenty of desserts, some for the guests who lingered, and we saved some for Peggy's arriving guests.

By 9:30, all the guests had left. At 10, the volunteers were leaving, happy but tired. Peggy's house was ready for her guests arriving the next day. We all agreed that at least two hundred people had attended.

The next day there was just over $48,000 counted with the online and checks contributions. It was so important that Roberta had trusted her intuition. I was so grateful that Peggy Hedberg had opened up her home a second time for Senator Obama. And the dedicated volunteers always did what needed to be done. That helped immensely to make the fundraisers ran smoothly behind the scenes. Volunteers invariably play a significant role in the success of fundraisers.

LESSON #9:

Honor those who came before.

Democratic Party of Wisconsin Open House

Thursday, February 12, 2009: 5:30 to 7:30 p.m.

King Street

Madison, Wisconsin

This fundraiser was a bit different than the previous ones; it was held after the presidential election and for the Democratic Party of Wisconsin (DPW). Still, I think it offers valuable insights. Personally, I learned additional skills working inside an established organization that was open to new ideas and solutions.

In late January 2009, I began a new job as the Democratic Party of Wisconsin's new finance director. The number of fundraisers I organized and the successes I had led to my hiring. I was given a date for my first fundraiser. I had three weeks to bring in $5,000.

Later, I found out my boss, Joe Wineke, the chair of the party, had thought that all my Obama supporters would come over and join the Democratic Party. While that made some sense, it never happened. The culture of the state party was different than the culture of the Obama campaign.

My second day, a friend came into the office and congratulated me on my new job. I shared my situation about the fundraiser in three weeks. I had no idea what was happening in state politics and who all the senators or assemblymen and women were. He offered ideas. One in particular sounded interesting and doable.

The state budget was presently a hot topic being discussed by the two majority leaders, Mark Miller in the Senate and Mark Pocan in the Assembly—names I did know. I had to get their personal contact information from the chair. It is against the state's campaign rules to do campaigning or fundraising inside the Capitol building. I called them, and they were excited about supporting the Party and were willing to do a presentation and update on the budget. I worked from my Obama list, the list of the Democratic Assembly and Senate members, and the Party's list. After conferring with the chair and the membership director, we decided on a $100 charge for sponsorships. Those names would be listed on the invitation. Twenty-five dollars would be the suggested donation at the door.

I did some quick arithmetic: thirty sponsorships and seventy-five with the $25 at the door totaled $4,875—close enough. Jamie knew a Democratic caterer that had called a while ago and wanted to donate to the Dems. I called the company and shared the expectation of a "strong" one hundred guests. I said that I could choose a date around their calendar. A Wednesday or Thursday evening sounded good. I chose Thursday. It gave me one more day for calls and organizing. We had a date.

I called Peter Leidy, a strong Dem who was also a gifted composer, singer, and guitarist. He was available on Thursday and would write a song for the fundraiser. What luck.

I made calls for sponsorships over the next few days. Then a strange thing happened. Former seven-term State Assemblywoman Midge Miller called me at home one night. She was widely known for her tenacity on many issues—the anti-war movement in Vietnam, women's rights, and bringing Senator Eugene McCarthy into the spotlight for the presidential race.

She spoke to me with great conviction. She was thrilled with Obama's presidential win. Then she abruptly said that hospice was at the door and hung up.

I called her son Senator Mark Miller the next day. Mark had already committed to the fundraiser. I told him about Midge's call and hospice.

He said, "Yes, Midge's cancer has returned." I told him about the loss of Rebecca Young and how her friends had not been able to thank her for all her work. I suggested that Midge could be a special guest at our event.

Mark knew that his mother would like the idea of being part of the Party's fundraiser. It was fitting; for so many years, she had advocated and passed state laws for Democratic issues. I went to the chair and explained the situation. Joe liked the idea and said okay. I called Mark to confirm.

About three months earlier, former and well-respected State Assemblywoman Rebecca Young had died from reoccurring cancer. Two weeks before, she had been testifying in a public meeting. When she passed away suddenly at home, her friends and colleagues from the county board and the school board grieved deeply, unable to say thank you for her service to the community. I didn't want that to happen to Midge and her wide circle of friends and activists.

Oddly, the next day Chair Joe Wineke said that he had just heard that another activist's cancer had returned too. Linda

Farley was a doctor who supported healthcare and social justice issues. She was Midge's friend. For years, they had worked together on fair housing issues.

Joe asked me to call their home. Linda's husband, Gene, also a doctor, answered. When I told him our idea, he said he wasn't too sure if she would enjoy being in the limelight; it wasn't her style. He wanted to think about it and talk to Linda. He would call back in a few days.

When Gene called back, both Farleys needed more persuasion. I talked about Rebecca Young's sad departure. Linda and Gene had known Rebecca. They would call Midge and let me know.

The next day, they agreed to join Midge as a special guest and were happy to do something for the Party. I added both Midge and Linda's names on a simple email invitation to a few hundred people. I called them "The Grand Dames of the Democratic Party."

The next morning, there were four unsolicited replies for $100 sponsorships, all to honor Midge and Linda. By the end of the day, with my calls to potential sponsors and more replies coming through the email, we had twelve sponsorships.

Two sponsors I called had known about Midge and Linda's cancer reoccurrences. I updated the chair with the number of confirmed sponsorships. He started to make calls to his high donor and union list. After ten days, we had thirty sponsorships. With a few days to go, I had a few more sponsorships come in. The chair was having a similar response. An announcement went out two days before the event with nearly forty sponsors, which stimulated more replies.

There was concern about filling a room that big. Several sponsors were from out of town and weren't sure if they would be attending. Also, I found out that many of the younger staff of the congressional politicians were accustomed to filling the room without contributing. The day before an event, the Party staff often called student friends and congressional staffers to fill the room.

I said, "Absolutely not," sharing two reasons with them. First, it would be disrespectful to those two extraordinary women activists.

I got back blank stares.

Did they know what these women had done for them?

They did not.

I told them about the contraceptive bill that had enabled women to get prescriptions at any pharmacy. That one significant bill convinced them. Weren't these women worth the cost of one or two beers? Secondly, how would they feel if they paid $25 or more, and the person next to them was eating and drinking for free? Would an annoyed person donate the next time the Party called?

They came around.

I could sense that there still was a problem. I had to keep the conversation going. Jamie and another staffer assigned to the fundraiser would be at the door collecting money. Then it occurred to me; how could they could say no to any friends who might show up expecting freebies? I put myself at the door, so everyone had to pass by me. I was the enforcer. They would take the money and register the people. On the day of the event, the staff and I were setting up the registration table at the entrance at the top of the stairs. The large room was cleared, and folding chairs lined its walls.

The speaker and microphone were checked. The glassed conference room with its large conference table was perfect for the food and drinks. The restroom was cleaned. The caterer confirmed the delivery time. He added 10 percent more food, drinks, plates, napkins and cups since the sponsors' list had grown to nearly ninety. We lined our office wastepaper baskets with plastic bags to protect them from the discarded food and drinks. We reserved seats so Midge and Linda had comfortable chairs at the front of the room, near the microphone.

People were already at the door when we opened it at 5:30 p.m. After twenty minutes, the oversized room was almost filled. I had to challenge some young people and ask for the cost of one or two beers. It worked. When the program started, there was a line down the stairs and into the street. We had hit capacity by the fire code. Many older people and state officials arrived on time to make sure they would have time to talk to both Midge and Linda.

A few minutes before the program, the chair asked Mark Miller and Mark Pocan to let Midge and Linda take over the microphone. He had talked to both Midge and Linda, and they liked the idea.

Peter's song got the attention of the audience of well over a hundred, with additional people standing in the entrance and stairs. The chair went to the microphone and made a smart decision. He said, "It looks like everyone here came to see Midge and Linda." He turned to the two Marks and joked about not giving the microphone to two politicians. Everyone laughed. "Tonight, this microphone is for Midge and Linda."

Both women had a grand time telling stories of their achievements, their disappointments, and surprises while working on issues and legislation.

I sent our young staffers at the registration table into the room to listen to Midge and Linda. I could manage the door. It was a memorable time.

After a good thirty minutes, the chair noticed Linda tiring out, and he ended the program. Many guests rushed to talk to them. An hour later, Midge was still talking. The food was nearly gone; just a few people remained. We started to clean up. Mark Miller slowly led Midge to the door. I was able to give her a big hug. She and Mark left with wide smiles.

Listening, being kind, and remembering to respect, empower, and include transformed this challenging event into the most successful fundraiser for the DPW than anyone could remember—or so said the chair at the program's end. For weeks, both the chair, staff, and I received thanks for doing the fundraiser with Midge and Linda. Midge and Linda's legacies had made it happen.

Midge died six weeks later. The chair, staff, and I attended Midge's memorial service. She had planned the service for a convenient time and place so many could attend. From my estimate, the packed church must have held at least three hundred family members, friends, cohorts, and admirers. Midge would have loved it. The service ended with a parade walking on the sidewalk to the Capitol grounds three blocks away. On the steps of the Capitol building, some politicians gave short speeches about Midge's days in the Assembly.

Linda passed away within four months—in her own style—with family and close friends. After serving in many different communities, much of her life had been devoted to lobbying for universal healthcare. She had received many awards for work and advocacy. After retiring from the University of Wisconsin Medical School, she volunteered her medical services to the communities in need.

She received a glimpse of hope for her efforts, witnessing President Obama announcing his effort for a better healthcare system in our country. **O**